A Life on Hold

Crossing Paths with Atrial Fibrillation

Kevin J. Kauffman

Printed in the United States of America.
ISBN: 1496199766
ISBN-13: 978-1496199768

FIRST EDITION

www.alifeonhold.com

Table of Contents

Appendix

INTRODUCTION

This book is written *by* an a-fib sufferer *for* the a-fib sufferer.
If you do not suffer from a heart arrhythmia, then much of
what lies within may mean little to you and could be difficult
to relate to. On the other hand, if you are not a sufferer
yourself but know or care for someone who is and struggle to
understand what they are going through on a daily basis,
then this book might help to shed some light on their ordeal.
As you read on, you will hear my personal story just as it
comes straight out of my head – complete with all of my
usual random thoughts and musings! It is the story of how
my life was so rudely interrupted by the most common, and
perhaps the most commonly overlooked (and maybe even
misdiagnosed) heart arrhythmia, atrial fibrillation. I will try
to convey to you my state of health before, during, and after
suffering from this condition as well as my own personal
perspective on the experiences of being diagnosed with,
living with, and then finally being free of atrial fibrillation.

Think of this book as a medical autobiography, of sorts. The facts and events that I recount herein are unembellished and entirely true and accurate to the best of my recollection. But please bear in mind that I am not a doctor (even though I may sometimes play one in real life!), nor do I have any formal medical background or training. And it is important to understand that the information and accounts that I present in this book are not, in any way, intended as advice and therefore should not be treated as such. All information in this book is provided "as is", without any representations or warranties, express or implied, and is not warranted to be complete, true, accurate, up-to-date, or non-misleading. You must not rely on this information as an alternative to or as a substitute for medical advice from a doctor or other professional healthcare provider. If you have specific questions or concerns about any medical matter, be sure to consult your doctor or another healthcare provider. If you think that you may be suffering from any medical condition, then you should seek medical attention immediately. Under no circumstances should you delay seeking medical advice, disregard medical advice, or discontinue treatments or therapies because of any information found in this book.

That being said, I sincerely hope that my story helps you to understand what you might be able to expect if you or someone you know is living with a condition such as a-fib or SVT. For those of you who are lucky enough not to know what these conditions are, let me offer a brief explanation. A-fib is the medical abbreviation for "atrial fibrillation" (see the *List of Acronyms* in the Appendix at the end of this book for many more relevant medical abbreviations). Atrial fibrillation is the most common type of heart arrhythmia and presently accounts for about one-third of all heart arrhythmia-related hospital admissions in the United States.

Fibrillation is a general term describing the rapid and unsynchronized or uncoordinated contraction of individual or small bundles of muscle fibers. In addition to the heart, fibrillation may also afflict skeletal muscles, in which case it is usually an indication of some type of pathology. This type of fibrillation should not be confused with fasciculation, which is a rapid but coordinated contraction of larger bundles of muscle fibers that usually present as twitches, which can often be felt and even seen if they occur close enough to the skin. Fasciculations generally have no pathological significance.

Fibrillation within skeletal muscles usually does not cause any problems for the sufferer. In fact, it is usually impossible to know that you even have it without visualizing the associated electrical activity with an electromyogram (a device similar to an electrocardiogram but used to measure the electrical activity of skeletal muscles rather than that of the heart muscle). When fibrillation happens in the heart, however, there is reason for concern. This is especially true when it occurs in the ventricles (the lower chambers of the heart). The right ventricle pumps oxygen-depleted blood to the lungs where it releases carbon dioxide and picks up fresh oxygen as it makes its way back to the heart where the left ventricle will then, ultimately, pump it out to all the tissues and organs throughout the rest of the body. If the muscle fibers in the ventricles fibrillate out of sync with each other rather than contracting rhythmically, these chambers fail to pump blood. I don't think I need to elaborate on why this is a very bad thing.

The atria (singular, "atrium") are the smaller, upper chambers of the heart. They sit atop the ventricles and serve a very different function. Simply put, the atria exist to allow a continuous and uninterrupted flow of blood throughout the body between ventricular beats. They serve as buffers, allowing venous blood to flow into the heart when the ventricles contract and pump blood out of the heart ("systole"). Then the atria squeeze the blood they've collected into the ventricles as the ventricles relax and expand between beats ("diastole"). The atria are very small, however, compared to the size of the ventricles, and the blood they pump into the ventricles accounts for only about 15% of the ventricles' total volume, so they are not essential to the actual pumping function of the heart. That is why fibrillation of the atria is <u>far</u> less dangerous than fibrillation of the ventricles. When the atria fibrillate, the sufferer can usually function normally with little to no (physical) ill effects, especially at rest. Although, the loss of that extra 15% of blood flow from the atria (known as the "atrial kick") can be noticeable to some as fatigue, dizziness, or shortness of breath, especially to the otherwise infirm or when under exertion or already suffering from physical exhaustion.

To be sure, though, there are some dangers that accompany atrial fibrillation, so you shouldn't just ignore it. But unlike the dangers of ventricular fibrillation, atrial fibrillation usually does not pose an immediate threat. One concern is that, when the heart spends enough time in continuous a-fib, a clot can form in the left atrium or, more likely, in the left atrial appendage (an offshoot of the left atrium within which blood can stagnate during periods when the atria are not contracting properly). If such a clot were to form, break free, and enter circulation, it could lodge in a blood vessel and cause a stroke or other damage elsewhere in the body. Doctors will often prescribe oral anticoagulant therapy in patients who suffer from very long bouts of a-fib to minimize the risk of developing such a clot and suffering a stroke.

Besides the possibility of one (relatively) large clot breaking free and causing a stroke, a long bout of a-fib can, theoretically, cause a stream of many very tiny clots to enter circulation. Clots of this size are unlikely to have any immediately noticeable effect anywhere in the body; however, it is thought (and has been shown with the use of electronic imaging) that these tiny clots can lodge in the smallest capillaries of the brain, blocking blood flow to very small groups of brain cells and damaging or killing them (these are known as "micro-infarcts"). The number of cells affected would, perhaps, be on the same order as those killed off by the proverbial night of heavy drinking and, unlike a stroke, would likely leave no immediate pronounced motor, sensory, or cognitive deficits in their wake. But the cumulative effect of many of these micro-events over time may account for some of the long-term cognitive symptoms witnessed in chronic a-fib sufferers – the worst-case scenario being full-blown dementia.

Another concern for atrial fibrillation sufferers is the long-term effect that the arrhythmia can have on the heart. The longer a-fib is left untreated, the more difficult it can be to treat. This is because the heart will often "remodel", or physiologically adapt to accept a-fib as its ersatz normal rhythm, making the heart less likely and less able to return to normal sinus rhythm ("NSR") on its own or possibly even in response to treatment with medications. A-fib also causes fibrosis (scarring) of the atrial muscles, which can ultimately adversely affect the sinoatrial (SA) node – the heart's natural pacemaker located on the right atrium. And if left to go on untreated even longer, the result can be cardiomyopathy (a broad term meaning a weakening of the heart muscle) and even congestive heart failure (inability of the heart to meet the blood flow needs of the body). Both of these are very serious conditions. So while the sufferer might not find the a-fib intrinsically bothersome, these are some compelling reasons for him to seek medical care and try to get it under control as soon as possible.

In addition to a-fib's direct effects on the heart, it can affect the sufferer in other ways, too. First, fibrillation of the atria causes an irregular ventricular rhythm. This is often felt as a twitching or jumping sensation in the chest, back, or neck (many describe it as "flopping fish" or "wrestling squirrels");

however, sometimes a-fib can be "silent" and go undetected until, for example, the radial (wrist) or carotid (neck) pulse is felt. This irregular pulse is often, but not always, rapid when in a-fib and can cause shortness of breath as the heart pumps less efficiently when beating at a high rate. The sensation alone can be quite unnerving, sometimes leading to anxiety, panic, and even long-term depression. And the rapid heart rate that often accompanies a-fib can also increase renal (kidney) function and cause frequent urination, a symptom that may then be further exacerbated by anxiety. Frequent urination, in turn, can result in dehydration and electrolyte imbalances that can also make the a-fib worse, cause other arrhythmias, or in extreme cases, damage the kidneys. Nausea and chest discomfort have also been reported with atrial fibrillation.

Many sufferers of a-fib also suffer from an unrelated but still-somehow-connected supraventricular tachyarrhythmia ("SVT"), properly named "atrial flutter" but also known as "a-flutter" or just "flutter". An SVT is a rapid ("tachy"), regular heart rhythm that originates above ("supra") the ventricles, or in other words, in the atria. (On a side note, the term "atrial tachycardia" is not used to describe these types of arrhythmias because that term was already in use to refer to one particular type of SVT, of which there are many.) Flutter is characterized by a rapid, regular pulse accompanied by a buzzing, humming, or vibrating sensation in the chest, back, or neck. This sensation comes from the very high rate of contraction of the atria.

In flutter, the atria contract at a rate that is an integer multiple of the ventricular rate (in a healthy heart, this multiple is usually two). The reason for this is that the atrioventricular ("AV") node – the electrical "connector" between the upper and lower chambers of the heart – takes a certain amount of time to "reset" after conducting an impulse from the atria to the ventricles. Any impulses coming in from the atria before the AV node resets are ignored (this is the AV node's "refractory period") and are not passed through to the ventricles. In this way, the AV node effectively "filters" dangerously fast rhythms coming from the atria. So if you measure your pulse in atrial flutter at 120 beats per minute, for example, then your atria would likely be contracting at a rate of 240, or twice as fast. It is this very high atrial rate that causes the buzzing sensation that is often associated with and is the hallmark of this particular type of SVT.

Atrial flutter comes in two "flavors" – right and left, named for the respective atrium in which each type originates. Right atrial flutter is the most common of the two, and it is typically the easiest to treat. It is often unstable, eventually degenerating into a-fib. But a-fib can also turn to or trigger atrial flutter, too. In fact, it is not uncommon to experience several to many alternating periods of each in a single episode. Right atrial flutter and a-fib can often be treated with many of the same medications. Left atrial flutter is an altogether different animal, however. It is unlikely to occur spontaneously (as a "lone" arrhythmia) and is most often seen as a "side effect", per se, of certain heart procedures or as a result of some sort of damage to the heart. It is more stable than right atrial flutter and therefore less likely to convert on its own, and it can be far more difficult to treat. Both types of atrial flutter carry the same risk of clots, cardiomyopathy, and atrial fibrosis as atrial fibrillation does, so it is important to get them treated, as well, even if they are not causing you any discomfort or adverse symptoms.

Volumes can be (and have been) written about atrial fibrillation and atrial flutter and their pathophysiologies, symptoms, treatments, etc. That is not my objective for this book, so I will leave it to the reader to do his/her own research. In fact, I highly encourage the atrial fibrillation and atrial flutter sufferers to educate themselves as much as possible on their conditions. Knowledge is our very best ally against the anxiety that often accompanies these and similar conditions that make you feel that you have lost control of your life. The better you understand, in general, what is going on under your skin, the less likely that it will scare you, and the better prepared you will be to combat it.

LIFE BEFORE A-FIB

Based on the feedback that I have elicited from members of this book's target demographic, I have decided to include these next two chapters giving a highly condensed overview of my life before atrial fibrillation set in and my complete medical history prior to my a-fib diagnosis. This chapter will give you a cursory understanding of me, my personality, and the life that has made me who I am. Knowing a little about my background, the decisions that I have made, and how I have chosen to live my life might help you to understand the thought processes behind the path that I have chosen with regard to my health care. To be honest, this is not the most interesting chapter – so by all means, feel free to skip it if you wish. But I do believe that this summary of my life may provide some insights into me and put the information presented in the rest of the book into a more meaningful perspective. Read it or don't... ultimately, that's entirely up to you. But don't ask me any questions about it if you don't!

So what better place to start than at the beginning? I am a child of the '60s, born in Pennsylvania somewhere between our state's capitol city, Harrisburg, and our nation's first capitol city, Philadelphia. I lived the first year of my life in an apartment that I have no memory of before moving to a semi-detached home in a nearby suburban neighborhood where I would spend most of the next two decades growing up. Ours was a typical working-class family – mom, dad, my younger brother who would come along a few years later, and me. Our mother left her paying job to toil thanklessly as our full-time caregiver and homemaker while our father worked his way up through the ranks (just as thanklessly, I might add) at one of our area's largest employers, a specialty steel manufacturer. We were situated less than a block away from the local fire company and our elementary school (which, by the way, was just razed after standing for nearly 100 years), and we spent a great deal of time playing in our back yard and on the school's playground and athletic fields, as did most of the other neighborhood kids.

Don't let that fool you, though... "playing outdoors" does not necessarily translate to "svelte and fit". Not even close. I was very uncoordinated and nonathletic, and I have always been overweight. I was a chubby baby and went on to sport size "husky" school clothes. Some may postulate that, because of my "strong" personality, I was quite a handful as a child, and that food may have been used to placate me when all other efforts failed. I cannot speak to the validity of this theory, but my present day love of food leads me to believe that it was nothing more than just that from the start. And as I got older, my love of food (and my interest in preparing it) grew. My mother was always very supportive whenever I wanted to step in to "soup up" her cooking with my own "secret blend" of spices (basically just a little of everything that I could find in the spice cabinet), however questionable the benefit over the original may have been. I really just loved the "kitchen chemistry" aspect of experimenting with ingredients and flavors. Success or failure, I'd never let any of it go to waste!

Although cooking was becoming somewhat of a hobby for me, the majority of my childhood interests lied in the realms of science and nature. I guess it was all but inevitable. My father was an outdoorsman, educated in chemistry and employed as a metallurgist in the steel industry. His father, my grandfather, owned a local TV and appliance sales and repair business (he sold the first televisions and installed the first TV antennas in our area) and on the side, doctored any and all wounded animals that he came across. We did our share of nursing infirm animals back to health in our home, too, and we had all sorts of animals as pets over the years – fish, birds, newts, lizards, salamanders, toads, crayfish, snakes, turtles, snails, mice, rats, hamsters, etc... everything but the usual dogs and cats. My dad started taking me fishing before I can even remember, my favorite part being scaring my mother with the worms that were fated to ultimately die as bait. But I also became fascinated with how the disembodied fish hearts would beat for hours in a bowl of salt water, and then when they eventually did stop, how I could sometimes restart them (at least for a little while) with a jolt of electricity from a battery. Little did I know how this was foreshadowing events to come later in my life.

But animals (and their anatomies!) were only a few of my many fascinations. My favorite TV show in 1972 was Don Herbert's "Mr. Wizard", and I asked for and received his namesake chemistry set for Christmas that year. My dad's idea to get it for me, I'm sure. Perhaps my parents were hoping to distract me from my unnatural interest in animal guts. Chemistry would remain a hobby of mine for years to come (though much to my parents' chagrin in many cases), but my true love quickly became electronics. It started with "helping" my grandfather in his shop, then I subscribed to Elementary Electronics magazine when I was seven or eight and received my first electronics project kit for my ninth birthday. My favorite project was not in the accompanying manual, though. It was a lawn chair "electric chair" that my friend and I dreamed up. We tricked my dad into being our guinea pig. He wasn't exactly angry that we tested it on him, but I don't think he like it very much, either. It should come as no surprise now to learn that my circle of friends consisted primarily of other local kids with inquisitive, albeit mischievous, minds. Hanging around with these kids led to my activities becoming even less athletic in nature and more akin to lab experiments. And, this shift toward the sedentary certainly did not help my weight situation at all.

Contrary to what you might assume, however, I was never a bookworm. Although I did enjoy looking through the World

Book® encyclopedias that our parents got for us when we were in elementary school, mining them for facts with which to fill my hungry mind (collectively referred to by my dad as "UBI", or "useless bits of information"). And in what would eventually reveal itself as another bit of foreshadowing, I compiled a "thesis" on the human heart and circulatory system over the summer break a year or two after we first got the encyclopedias. It was not a project for school, just for my own edification. It was complete with diagrams, charts, drawings, and all the facts (definitely A-quality work!). But after exhausting the resources at my disposal (one encyclopedia), my passing interest in the heart had waned. I did build a pumping heart model several years later while I was going through a "model building" phase, but most of my time indoors was spent in our basement at my little gray workbench that my dad had cobbled together for me out of miscellaneous wood scraps.

When down in my "workshop", I especially liked to try to "fix" things. If it didn't work, I couldn't wait to get my hands on it. Looking back, though, it's evident that most of these things that I fixed (a lot of kitchen appliances) only needed fixing because I took them apart or otherwise broke them somehow in the first place. I usually managed to get them back together, even though there were sometimes a few parts left over. But those parts were usually not very important anyway. In that same vein of mechanical aptitude, I also enjoyed designing and building things in my workshop. After all, I had to find a use for all those leftover parts! But my favorite basement pastime was to design and perform experiments. These experiments usually involved chemicals and/or electricity. Both types were equally unsafe, and with outcomes equally as undesirable (at least for my parents)... and even worse when both were used at the same time. But a negative result is still a result, right?

In school, math and science were my best subjects – rarely did I not ace these classes, and I really did enjoy them. English and social studies, however, fell far at the other end of the spectrum. I loathed them. Just the idea of reading and doing book reports made me physically ill. And I saw no point in memorizing the uninteresting facts doled out in social studies. Make no mistake, my sentiment for these classes was clearly reflected in my grades. But I somehow always managed to squeak by in the end. Maybe my teachers saw a glimmer of promise in me through my math and science grades and cut me a little slack. I might have been the first kid not left behind!

By sixth grade, my arguably high IQ score had landed me in my school district's newly-instituted educational enrichment program along with a handful of other students from throughout the district. If I remember correctly, we met one day every week (something that one of my regular teachers absolutely despised), and we worked on lots of fun hands-on projects... it was much better than real school! The lot of us went on to become the so-called "gifted" section in junior high school, and we pretty much stuck with each other from class to class, year after year, for the next three years, leaving little opportunity to meet other students and make new friends outside of this exclusive group. This was especially true for someone like me with no athletic abilities whatsoever who did not participate in many extracurricular activities besides a few nerdy clubs that consisted mostly of other kids already in my section.

OK, that's not entirely true. I was in the "Y Indian Guides" at age seven – it was an outdoor community-building fellowship program for boys and their fathers sponsored by the YMCA. At age eight, I joined the Cub Scouts, and I stuck with that all the way through the first year of Boy Scouts. I wasn't very well-received in the Boy Scouts, so I joined the Explorers (a vocationally-oriented branch of the Boy Scouts) instead. I also played intramural soccer for a few years in elementary school (the fat kid always has to play goalie, of course) and some intramural volleyball in junior high. I participated in some geeky groups in junior high, too – the fun math club, the model rocket club, and the AV club.

Things were quite different in high school, though. Different faces in every class, some who I didn't know at all who came up from the other junior high school in our district. My one "constant", however, during my three years of high school was the TV Crew. Several of my junior high school friends joined this club, too, and I had met a few guys a year or two older than me who were already in the TV Crew in the electronics and computer Explorers post that I had joined over the summer before I started high school. For the next three years, nearly all of my time was spent either in the TV

Crew's TV studio or working at TV Crew functions... during school, after school, and even over the summer. It was technical, geeky, social, involved working with electronics, and I found it very cool to be part of and to have my name in the credits of our live weekly news and sports broadcasts on our local cable network. Plus, it proved a fine distraction from English and social studies!

Before I even started high school, I really thought I wanted to take classes at our district's vocational/technical school in lieu of preparing for college. My guidance counselor felt strongly otherwise, though, and talked me out of it, saying that I was placed in the gifted section in junior high school for the specific reason of preparing me for college. So I took her direction and signed up for all the high school college-prep classes. I took the NMSQT and SATs when they were offered, and when the time came in my senior year, I talked to my counselor about applying to colleges. After all, this is what was expected of me. But I still really felt like I just wanted to go to a technical school and then get out in the real world and get right into some hands-on work. Once again, though, I was talked out of it by several of my teachers who I knew on a less formal level. They all felt that technical school would be a waste of my intelligence and that I should go to college.

So again, doing as was expected of me, I contacted a bunch of the big science and engineering colleges, got their brochures in the mail, read them, and picked out a few that looked as though they might be interesting to pursue. I figured that, if

I was going to go to college, then I would major in electrical engineering. I still had a great deal of interest in electronics (from those days in my grandfather's shop), but my real hope was that, as an engineer, I could save up enough money to eventually open my own restaurant... a little backward, maybe? It made sense to me at the time. I probably should have gone to culinary school instead... but hindsight is always 20/20, isn't it?

Being torn between four more very expensive years of school and two more less expensive years of school, and not being certain if I even wanted to go to college, I waited until three months *after* all the colleges' application deadlines had passed before sending off my one and only application. It was to Lehigh University in Bethlehem, Pennsylvania. I picked Lehigh because it was relatively close to my home compared to the other schools that I had considered, my dad was sent there by his employer on several occasions to take some classes, and I had been there once for a National Honor Society event, so the campus was not completely unfamiliar to me. But the main reason that I applied there was because I knew that it was a very difficult school to get into, and since I was submitting my application so late and without the required ACT results or essay, I was certain that I would have no chance of being accepted. And that's just what I wanted!

Well, guess again. Much to my surprise, I was invited to join Lehigh University's next freshman class. I guess my SAT scores were too high for them to pass up... well, they were over Lehigh's minimum requirement for the college of engineering, anyway. Also to my surprise, I was not upset by the fact that I was accepted. I was excited. Looking back, all that time that I thought that I did not want to go to college, I was probably just afraid of wanting to get in but being rejected – a theme that, on a side note, would persist through much of my life and that sadly holds many people back from realizing their full potential. But now I had to mentally prepare myself for four more years of school and for living on my own. I had to jump through the proverbial hoops, too, trying to grab as much of the sorely-needed scholarship and financial aid money as I could get my hands on. And my anticipation grew.

Once in college, I did a lot of growing up – in both the emotional and physical senses. College was more difficult, more fun, more intense, more free, more everything than I could have ever expected it to be. I had to learn to coexist with other smart-alecks in a sea of big egos and clashing personalities. I had to manage money and time and learn to control my impulses and whims. I joined a newly-colonized fraternity and rose through the ranks of committee chairs and various offices up to and including President, and I even sat on the board of directors of our fraternity's house-holding corporation. In these positions, I found myself going up against the administration of the university over various matters and juggling that with school work, a job, and other commitments. I was forced to deal with things such as housing problems, unscrupulous landlords, police response to noise complaints, underage drinking, drug use, insurance claims, social relationships, and other real world situations, all while striving to adhere to the strict guidelines of, and meet the high standards of, our fraternity's national chapter. In a very big way, the experience that I received from fraternity life had more practical application to me, moving forward, than the textbook education that I received over my four years of college (the details of which, you will notice, I have just spared you!).

In addition to the emotional challenges that I faced in college, subsisting on a diet consisting largely of salty, fatty junk food and cheap beer during this time contributed significantly to an almost 60-pound weight gain over the first three and a half years. Yes, I was aware that I had been putting on some weight, but it wasn't until I weighed in for intramural tug-of-war in November of my senior year that I learned (with much shock and awe) just how much. I may have even gained a few more pounds over that following Thanksgiving and winter breaks, too. And by the time I returned to campus in January for the spring semester, I could barely walk to class without seeing spots and feeling like I was going to pass out. I knew that I needed to get back into shape for on-campus interviews that were coming up in March, so I tossed the junk food to the masses, swore off all beer, and began a diet of mostly fruit with just a few ounces of protein per day... and lots of water. Lehigh's campus was on a hill, and our fraternity house was several blocks below campus, so between the diet plan that I held myself to and just walking to and from class (and everywhere else, for that matter, as I had no car), the weight came off... fast! Being only in my 20s had a lot to do with it, too, I'm sure. I felt so much better getting back to my "normal" level of overweight, and although I gave up the strict diet after dropping the weight, I was able to keep up a relatively healthy lifestyle for many years to come.

Also while in college, I developed a surprising interest in music. Several of my friends had started a band back at home around that time, and a few of my fraternity brothers had guitars, too – two of whom were also in a band. I started to think that I might like to try to play guitar, too. Why not! I even had a professor who was in a band. Not surprising that many of the senior projects built for his class were music-oriented. My project? An electronic drum synthesizer. It may not have been the most complex project, but it worked really well and did earn my lab partner and me a solid A in the class. Perhaps that also had something to do with the poem that we included at the end of the report ("An Ode to Senior Lab"). Writing poetry... another surprising interest that I had developed during my college years.

Back to the subject of guitars, though. It was when one of my fraternity brothers gave me an old Marvel arch-top with a completely severed neck that I knew that my dream would be realized. Doing what I do best, I "fixed" it... and then I made it better by adding a homemade electric pickup and connected it to a salvaged tape deck amplifier feeding an <u>old</u> schoolhouse-style paging speaker (complete with original wooden enclosure). But that wasn't enough. Rock was my genre, so my guitar needed distortion. Poor college student that I was, my only option, as I saw it, was to build my own "fuzz box". It was of my own design, and I really did not quite know what I was doing, but the whole setup actually worked fairly well. And when the entrepreneurial spirit hit me years later, I considered making a business out of this device. Actually, I have not yet totally abandoned this idea... I guess I'm still not sure what I want to do when I grow up!

I was luckier than some to have had a well-paying job lined up to start right after graduation – thanks in no small way to a sudden thunderstorm that struck as I was walking across campus back from my very last final exam of my senior year. It forced me to duck into the closest university building where I happened to spot a job posting on a bulletin board. An engineering job. Not exactly my ideal job, but it was in New Jersey, only 20 miles from campus. This allowed me to continue to live the college life with my fraternity brothers... and earn a salary at the same time! I worked there with a few other guys right out of college, and even though most of the work itself was boring, it was a comfortable and fun place to work. I gained valuable experience dealing with peers and management and battling the union mindset, and I gained insight into electronics manufacturing, shop floor control, and inventory control that would serve me well in my next job (which, unbeknownst to me at the time, was not far off).

The company that I worked for in NJ was poorly managed and had recently made some overambitious acquisitions. It was on its way out before I was even hired, and after just one year, my position was eliminated along with countless others. My termination came at a time when two of the other guys and I were considering leaving anyway to start our own computer business (not a whole lot of competition in the computer field in 1989!). Had the corporate job held out a little longer, we may have actually gone through with it. One of the guys did eventually see our plan through and was very successful in the field (I am sure many of you were familiar with his brand). With heavy college debt hanging over my head, though, I was anxious just to find a new regular job with a steady income. So I cut my expenses by temporarily moving back in with my parents while spending the next nine months job hunting by day and going out every night – either for happy hour, to catch some live music, or working lights and sound for my friends' band.

The new job that I finally landed filled a vacancy in the engineering department of a very small local electronics manufacturer and repair shop. At first glance, they seemed to be going nowhere, with competent employees but internal conflict pulling them in different directions. And the starting pay was poor... significantly less than that of my previous job. But the benefits were good, and the work did seem much more interesting than the job that I just left, and within the first year, I had received several pay increases, and the company had grown significantly. It was obvious to me then that they were actually on their way up, and as I learned more about their philosophies and methods of operation, I began to develop a new found respect for management. Finally able to buy my first new car, I was willing to hang in there a little longer to see where it went. Of course, as a small company, we each wore several hats throughout the typical work day, which could get hectic at times. But it also meant that we were each more free to do our jobs as we saw fit. And as an independent thinker, this was a very important factor for me to consider.

Sticking with this job would soon lead to several milestones in my life. One was on the social front. While I knew quite a few people from my college years and from my previous job, we were more "friends by contact", drawn together by shared circumstance. Whenever I thought of "going out", though, it was with the friends that I had back at home. At this job, however, I pushed myself to go out with some of the people there and get to know them outside of work, and I expanded my circle of friends for the first time, well... ever. Career-wise, in just a few short years and not by virtue of any prior formal experience – only through my willingness to learn and do – I found myself in the position of IT Manager, responsible for the entire corporation's network infrastructure, computers, databases, software, website, and phone system. The lessons learned from these personal growth events would be the first two of four major driving factors that would mold me into the person that I was to become over the next 20 years, the person that I am today.

My career with that company lasted just over 15 years. I saw the business grow from 15 employees stationed in an ill-fitting leased office space and with annual revenues of only a couple hundred-thousand dollars to nearly 200 employees between two locations – an 80,000 square foot corporate headquarters and a remote satellite manufacturing facility – with annual revenues approaching forty million dollars. As we grew, I was charged with developing custom software and network and telecom infrastructure to facilitate the growth as well as with implementing the policies and procedures surrounding them, many of which, at least in part, still dictate the operations of that company to this day.

I took that job very seriously, spending many a night working late to ensure successful backups and smooth operations for the early-rising manufacturing crew the following morning and also performing software upgrades and maintenance after hours and over weekends to avoid disrupting business. While the pay was good – enabling me to buy two new cars and my first house – it was not great with respect to the position that I held and its responsibilities. But I was trusted and left on my own, largely unsupervised, to do what I felt was best in the manner in which I chose. That meant more to me than money. I took great pride in my work and continuously strove to improve everything that I could, even getting just a fraction of a percent of additional efficiency out of a business process made the long hours worthwhile.

For most of the last 11 years at this job, I was a one-man department, and as such, I rarely found time to take any time off for myself or even to have much of a personal life at all. Several long-term relationships came and went during this period, and my "vacations" were largely limited to just a single day off here and there either to go golfing or to spend a long weekend with friends. And when I did get a day off, I always knew that there would be a lynch mob waiting for me when I got back to the office. Hiring an assistant in my last few years helped some, but even on my days off, I often ended up on the phone trying to solve problems remotely... usually more trouble than it was worth! So even though I did take a little more time off during those last few years, I rarely felt comfortable taking more than just a day at a time.

Regardless of the job's downside, I might still be with that company today had it not been for my father's sudden and unexpected death in 2003. This was the third pivotal event that would drive me on to be who I am today. It made me look back at my dad's life – proudly working 35 years for the same company just to be demoted and degraded by a new supervisor in an attempt to coerce him to quit so they could replace him with someone younger and more degreed... someone, ironically, who he would be tasked with training to replace him. He hung in there long enough to retire, all the while watching his long-time co-workers and friends lose their jobs, being let go for the same purpose over petty, contrived infractions. Once my dad did retire, he began suffering the loss of beloved family members – one right after the other. He had been looking forward to spending time with these family members in his retirement, but instead he was attending their funerals. It left him miserable, depressed, and full of regret. His subsequent untimely demise made me realize that none of us know how long we have here on this Earth, and I vowed to take action in my own life to ensure that I would not have any regrets of my own at the end of the ride.

Another consequence of my father's passing was that his responsibility of looking after his father, my then 90-year-old grandfather who had been living alone for a couple of years since my grandmother's passing, was then passed down to me. (By the way, my grandfather was diagnosed with an atrial arrhythmia at age 17 and lived with it for almost 78 years with no treatment at all. He'd simply lie down and perform carotid massage whenever a bout struck). I had always looked up to my grandfather for leaving his job at a very young age, not long after my father was born, and starting his own business with my grandmother. They were very successful and were able to live a comfortable life and take trips all around the world. As they got older, not long after they retired (a time when you would expect people to start traveling even more), they began staying at home most of the time. Going out for dinner every night was just about their only luxury. When I asked them about it, they said that they'd already seen everything they'd ever wanted to see.

Fair enough. It wasn't like they were sitting around the house, bored – my grandmother loved her gardening, and my grandfather enjoyed the repairs and maintenance that came with home and car ownership. And he also had his prized possession to keep him busy – his homemade one-seat car that he built from scratch in the 1940s. He was a local celebrity because of this car (and even got on national TV with it), and now that I was seeing him one-on-one much more often than ever before, I got to learn so much more about the car's history and his life, in general. He passed away in 2008, just two months before his 95th birthday, and it was his wish for his car to be put on public display for all to see. What better way to do this than to put it on the Internet? So I gave it its own website and Facebook page (the car itself waits in my garage for its moment to reemerge). My grandfather truly had no regrets, and if I could have a life only half as good as his, I would be very happy.

The one thing that I have always wanted but never pursued was to own a restaurant or to somehow be involved in a food service business. In 2002, I started making and selling hot sauce and seasonings. But I ran it as a side business in what little spare time that I had. I did not have the confidence to quit my corporate job to run it full-time, so it never went very far. I made up my mind, though, that I would somehow pursue this passion of mine some day. I did not know exactly how or when, but I was already taking evening classes at a local Small Business Development Center at that time, and I decided to check with our local Chamber of Commerce. They signed me up for a new Entrepreneur Support Program that they just started. Through it, I got limited accounting and legal counseling free of charge and general guidance on starting a business. In the end, the amount of money that I would have needed to open even a small restaurant, though, was still far beyond what I could come up with at that time.

But just when the restaurant idea had been moved to the back burner, I met a woman (a former high school classmate) who had already opened and operated several of her own restaurants in a neighboring town. We began dating and looked into opening a restaurant together. Again, the money was the biggest stumbling block. So we began thinking smaller, and then even smaller, and the idea of a mobile food trailer began looking like the most feasible option. We had lined up several venues that might work and had picked out a suitable trailer and a van to haul it, designed a menu, etc. Then as most relationships do, ours came to an end. And so did the business idea. But I had already decide to set the wheels in motion at my corporate job and gave them my one year's notice. I began cashing in my 1,000+ hours of accrued vacation time, and I even hired a new assistant who I was training to take over for me when I left. Yes, just like my dad, I was training him myself. But this was different... I was doing this on my own terms.

When that one year was up, I said my goodbyes. Of course, as it so often happens, I spent the next year or more consulting for my former employer, but most of those first five months were spent shopping for food trailers and vehicles (when I wasn't building a tree house "man cave" with two of my buddies – fueled by what seemed like beer, alone). In the process of searching, I came across some food trucks. This was at least five years before the food truck craze really began to catch on, so it seemed like a foreign concept at the time. But I contacted the seller of one in particular that caught my eye, and we spoke for almost an hour. The truck and the business sounded great, and the price was right. But I had to take a look at this truck first. It was in Niagara Falls.

I set out on the eight-hour drive very early one morning, checked out the truck, test drove it, and talked to the guy for a while. And then just two hours after arriving, I put down a deposit and made the eight-hour drive back home. The next day, still exhausted from my insane journey the day before, I made all the necessary insurance and title transfer arrangements, and the following week, I took an overnight bus trip back up to Niagara Falls (the events, sights, and experiences of which could comprise an entire book in itself!). The bus dropped me off around 8:00 a.m., and the seller of the food truck picked me up and took me out for breakfast. This would be the first time in my life that I ever drank coffee. We both figured I would need it – and lots of it – for a nine-hour drive home following a long night of no sleep at all on the bus. Yes, the return trip would take nine hours because the truck's seat was permanently fixed in an uncomfortable 90° position very close to the steering wheel, and I took a short break every hour to get out and stretch. I don't remember how much coffee I had at the restaurant, but it seemed like a lot. It wasn't as bad as I thought it would be, either (especially with lots of sugar!). So I got a big cup to go before we left, went back to the seller's home to get the truck, switched license plates, and then I hit the road. I made it home just in time for one of my friend's to pick me up to take me to a poker game at another friend's house that night... where, instead of the usual beer, I needed even more coffee just to stay awake! I was not the big winner that night.

Over the following weeks and months, I had the graphics on the truck changed, made quite a few modifications and upgrades to the interior, and got it inspected and licensed for food service. I put up a website and printed brochures and business cards and began advertising. Enter the cruel hand of Fate... just as I was booking my first event with the food truck, the woman who I originally collaborated with to get into the business, the one who I broke up with almost two years earlier, contacted me with a proposal to help her with the opening of a new restaurant. After much (clouded) consideration, I accepted and offered as much help as I could while still trying to my own new business off the ground. There was a lot of physical labor involved on both fronts, and after just a few months working both of these jobs, I was probably in the best physical condition of my life. Seriously.

Then I decided it was best that I became an official, legal partner in the restaurant venture that I was putting so much time into, after which I began devoting even more of my time and most of money toward renovating the building that we had leased. But then, after another couple of months of hard work and with a laundry list of expenses paid, the partnership went sour (to put it nicely). I was forced out of the business and lost my considerable investment. I soon became embroiled in legal (in)action over recouping my losses, which, unfortunately but not unexpectedly, never happened. The lawyer told me to simply write it off as a bad investment and move on. But I had become consumed with the whole ugly matter and found it difficult to let go. I was angry and depressed, and I let my own business fall even more by the wayside. I did eventually pull through, but for a while it was a period of great stress for me – possibly the most stress that I had ever been through in my entire life. And I am certain that my then-uncontrolled blood pressure was quite high throughout all of it.

Before it all fell through, though, while I was still renovating the restaurant, I was in the habit of eating breakfast every day. That is something that I normally hardly ever do. We'd go to a diner just down the street, and I'd almost always get some form of coffee. Because I was waking up earlier than usual every day, I felt that I needed it. Then even after I was no longer involved in the restaurant, as the colder months set in, I'd break out this old coffee maker that I had stored away for I don't even know how many years – one of those freebies that you get when you buy a sample of the coffee (you've seen the offers). I thought it would be good to have around just in case someone would come by and wanted coffee. Remember, it was only the year before that I had acquired a bit of a taste for coffee after my long trip to pick up the food truck, so this machine had probably never been used at this point. I even still had the vacuum sealed foil bags of coffee that I had to buy with the machine, too. So now, as winter approached and the days got colder, I'd occasionally brew up a pot and have a cup or two. And when I came down with a cold about this time, I added a new stimulant-based nasal decongestant spray that a friend had recommended to my usual regimen of oral antihistamines and decongestants. I had been in the habit of taking these for the past thirty years, but the spray was the proverbial straw that broke the camel's back, and my first bout of what was to become chronic atrial fibrillation set in.

Meanwhile, my food truck's water system had to be winterized and therefore could not operate in the sub-freezing temperatures. So the most that I could do over the winter was to use the truck as my kitchen for catering while it was parked in my driveway. My a-fib worsened all the while, and when the weather finally warmed up and I began booking some new events, I found that the effects of the arrhythmia had made it very difficult for me to handle most of the work. I scaled the business back to only catering and left the truck parked in my driveway where I kept it licensed and inspected as my company's kitchen. Business was very slow, though, and I soon had to shut it down altogether and fall back on what I did best... IT (a.k.a. computer stuff).

I began working as a freelance small business computer consultant and website designer. That business was doing well, and I realized I would soon need a better office than the spare bedroom that I had been using. I needed an office that was accessible from outside with enough room to meet with clients. So I undertook the conversion of half of my two-car garage into my new office. The worsening a-fib and the medications that I was on made the work difficult at times, but after three months, the office was finished, and sadly, it was time to sell the food truck. It was three more months before I found a buyer, but I got back my full investment and more, and the transaction took away a lot of stress with it. But my a-fib continued to march on and take over my life.

Around this time, I was still able to kick off another venture (in between bouts of a-fib, of course). It was to first design and build a greywater recycling system for my home and then draw up construction plans for it and publish them for sale. It would be a system constructed using only readily available, off-the-shelf components. In a few weekends and after a little tweaking, it worked great and significantly cut my water consumption over the ensuing months. The next step was to compile the plans. Then I created a website and made a Facebook page that have reached thousands of interested parties around the world with hundreds of sets of plans sold to customers mostly from Africa, the Middle East, and Australia. On several occasions, I was invited to consult on larger commercial installation projects and to speak or give demonstrations at colleges and "green living" conferences and consortia. But as all these would have involved more-or-less extensive travel, I always felt that I had to decline due to my health concerns.

Later this same year, a concerned friend made me promise to see a doctor about my degenerating condition, which, at this point, I had let go, untreated, for almost two years. I kept my word, saw a doctor, started medications, and then the side effects began. The a-fib continued to worsen, my quality of life declined, as did my ability to perform my job. After another year of this misery, surgery brought a brief period of relief, during which I tried to get back to normal. But the arrhythmia came back after a few months and was worse than ever. I became good at ignoring it by now, but the lack of sleep turned me into a "zombie". I tried more medications that didn't work. And then, an ischemic cerebrovascular event – the jury's still out on whether it was a stroke or a transient ischemic attack ("TIA") – compelled me to elect a second surgery, this time a virtual cure... for me, anyway. So far. Only time will tell.

All of this a-fib nonsense had consumed more than five years of my life. I was feeling significantly better after the second surgery, but I now suffered from the side effects of medications, and I still carried a great deal of extra weight that I gained from the a-fib. Most of the weight came off fairly quickly, as before, but the side-effects persisted (as some of them still do). Life never did quite get back to where I had hoped it would. Business has picked up, but because of some of the health issues that persist to this day, I have not felt comfortable pursuing certain opportunities that arise, taking some trips that I had planned, or getting involved in anything more than just casual social relationships. Of course, the longer I live alone, the harder it is to imagine ever being able to tolerate sharing my space with someone else (and vice versa!), so the latter has really becoming a non-issue.

My struggle on the cardiac front has certainly shifted my focus away from any personal goals that I may have once had. Now I feel better concentrating my efforts on helping others with the knowledge and experience that I have gained through my ordeal – just my way of trying to turn life's lemons into lemonade, I guess. I have become an active counselor of fellow a-fibbers – in person, by phone, via email, and online. I am also involved with several domestic health advocacy organizations and have participated in national focus groups and discussion panels on various health-related subjects. And at the time of writing, I am planning to attend an invitation-only national consortium for select online atrial fibrillation activists and healthcare professionals... we are just waiting for the sponsors to work out the financial details. And if they can't do it soon, I may start looking into what it would take to put one together on my own. It seems like too good of an idea not to do it.

It is my commitment to this new-found mission, and the encouragement of my many fellow a-fibbers who look to me for answers, opinions, and/or attitudes (you can rest assured that you will always get at least one of these from me!) that have spurred me on to compile this book from the accidental education that I have received through my brush with atrial fibrillation – through conversations with dozens of patients, doctors, and others in the medical field, research that I have done on my own, and the piles of data and personal notes that I have collected and compiled pertaining to my own case. I sincerely hope that you find at least something in here that is of some value to you.

My Medical History

This chapter should prove a little more relevant than the last, and I believe that it will cover information that is much more germane to the central topic of this book – the heart arrhythmias that I will eventually develop later in my life. This material is fairly important, I think, so I hope you will be able to relate to at least a few of the things that I mention here. It is my goal to list every health-related issue and event throughout my life that I can remember, and I have arbitrarily decided to arrange them by where on the body they occur starting with my head and proceeding downward. There is also a chronological summary of the main bullet points at the end of the chapter for those who wish to save some time and forgo the details.

OK, let's take it from the top... my head. Headaches. I started complaining of headaches at about age five or six. I am not sure if my headaches were any worse than those of any other average kid of that age or if I just complained about them more, but my parents did the right thing by consulting my pediatrician. He thought they were probably related to sinus inflammation or congestion. I remember using the steam vaporizer quite a bit after that, and I took acetaminophen (Tylenol®) because at that time we thought that I was allergic to aspirin (you may know it as "ASA", or "acetyl salicylic acid"). When the headaches continued to worsen, though, my parents were referred to an otolaryngologist (also known as an "ENT" for "ear, nose, and throat" doctor).

I was about nine years old when I first saw the ENT. My diagnosis was sinus inflammation and congestion, and a head x-ray showed a polyp in my nasal cavity. I don't remember exactly where it was (I don't think I even got to see the x-ray), but if I had to guess, I would say that it might have been in the right maxillary sinus – a hollow cavity in the bone to the right of the nose, spanning from just above the upper jaw to just below the eye socket. The polyp was insignificantly small at the time, but years later when I was in 11th grade I would develop a sudden and very bad pressure within this same sinus cavity accompanied by pain that was almost unbearable. It was so bad that I had missed some school because of it (and I rarely ever missed school). My family doctor gave me a sample of a very powerful prescription decongestant, and just one single dose opened up the sinus and allowed it to drain, no antibiotics needed. I am not sure whether it was the same polyp that caused this event (and countless other similar but less severe issues that I had before and since that time), but I do believe it is likely... especially given the most recent imaging that I have had done of the inside of my head. But more on that later.

I also suffered from nasal allergies as a child, and my doctor recommended that I take an over-the-counter antihistamine for them – chlorpheniramine (Chlor-Trimeton®). It was not very effective as I recall, but I continued to take it, especially after the sinus diagnosis, because it was available in a combination tablet with the decongestant, phenylpropanol-amine, or PPA (sold as Allerest®, among others). By the way, if you think you recognize the acronym PPA, it's because it was widely used in various over-the-counter cold medicines, stimulants, and weight loss products, and there were numerous reports in the news linking it to increased stroke risk in young people. Because of this danger, the FDA advised against its manufacture and use in the year 2000 and then, just a few years later, banned it from over-the-counter sale (it was also commonly used in the illegal manufacture of amphetamines). I discontinued my use of this decongestant long before then, though, because the chlorpheniramine was no longer very effective against my allergies. I had switched to taking diphenhydramine (Benadryl®) for my allergies and pseudoephadrine (Sudafed®) in a separate tablet for my nasal and sinus congestion. I was on a steady diet of these for many years. The sale of pseudoephadrine, by the way, was also restricted in 2006 because of its increasing use in the manufacture of illegal amphetamines.

Not long after seeing the ENT, around age nine or ten, and because of the increasing severity of my allergies, I went to see an allergist for the classic pin prick test. An array of what seemed like a hundred liquid allergen droplets was laid out on my back, and then the skin under each droplet was pricked with a pin. After that, I just lied there on the table waiting for the swelling and itching to begin. Nearly every one of the allergens reacted, or at least it felt that way. Tree, grass, weed, and flower pollens, house dust, and cats. I also had two lines of six subcutaneous injections of allergen serums on my forearm. Every one of these swelled like huge hives. The worst part of the test was going back to school that afternoon with calamine lotion all over my arm and my back, itching so badly that I couldn't sit still in my chair. The test really didn't do much good because the prescribed treatment for these allergies was an oral antihistamine, which I was already taking. I guess I could have opted for regular allergy shots, but my symptoms were really not that severe. Looking back, though, had I opted for the shots in lieu of many years of allergy and sinus meds, it may have retarded the development of some of my other health issues.

In addition to the nasal allergies, I also suffered from severe contact dermatitis and some food/drug allergies. Just about every green plant gave me a rash similar to poison ivy if I came in contact with it. That didn't stop me from being a kid and playing in the grass, but I always paid for it later. The same thing happened when I came into contact with dusty or dirty surfaces, especially outdoors (probably due to pollen). The only treatment for this rash at that time was an expensive prescription steroid-based cream. Later, over-the-counter hydrocortisone creams would become available, but they were far less effective. The only "treatment" for the food and drug allergies was to avoid the offending substance... the most difficult of these being chocolate. I did grow to like carob, though, which *looks* similar to chocolate but tastes nothing at all like it. Even better than carob, however, was white chocolate. And even though my chocolate allergy was limited to my prepubescent years, I still don't have much of a taste for chocolate even today and usually prefer white chocolate when given the choice.

The drug allergy that I referred to was to aspirin. At least that's what I thought for most of my life. My pediatrician made the diagnosis when I was just a baby. I broke out in hives after taking chewable baby aspirin for a fever that I had with a cold. Doctors now know that hives can accompany viral infections, especially in infants, and that aspirin may exacerbate this effect – it is not necessarily a sign of an allergic reaction. An allergy test for aspirin many years later would bear this out, but without knowing this, I was sentenced to half a lifetime of taking nothing but largely ineffective acetaminophen for pain and fever. I stayed away from all other NSAIDs (non-steroidal anti-inflammatory drugs) because they all carried the warning to avoid them if you are allergic to aspirin. It wasn't until another doctor told me many years later that, even if I *were* allergic to aspirin, ibuprofen would probably be safe to take. I tried it (with Benadryl® close by), and I had no adverse reaction to it. Finally, I could take a pain killer that actually worked!

Moving on in the head area, we come to my eyes. One of the most vivid memories of my childhood is that it seemed like I always had a case of conjunctivitis ("pink eye"), and that I always needed to use a painful antibiotic eye drop to get rid of it. Besides that, my vision checked out at 20/20 or better every year when we were tested in school, that is until I reached puberty... that's when everything changes! After my doctor checked my eyes during a regular exam, he recommended that I see an eye doctor. The eye doctor found no problems with my eyes besides myopia (near-sightedness). My mother and brother both already wore glasses for this condition, but it wasn't until more than six years later that I would first don my own corrective eyewear.

On to my mouth and throat. My mandibular deciduous teeth (lower baby teeth) were very crowded, and there was concern over whether there would be enough room for my permanent teeth once they started coming in. But when one of the central incisors came out and there was no permanent tooth beneath it, the gap left just enough room for the rest of my teeth to spread out evenly. My molars still came in very crooked and had very deep crevices at the intersections of the individual cusps. It was impossible to clean these teeth properly, so they had to be sealed with a UV-cured polymer as soon as they erupted to prevent inevitable decay down the line. Or at least my dentist had us believing this. He also felt that I should have braces on them so I could chew properly (but it is obvious by looking at me that I have always been able to chew just fine!). The sealing treatment was relatively new, and it was expensive. So were braces. I skipped the braces since my visible teeth were straight, and I just had the sealing done – once on each tooth as it came in. This spanned two years when I was about eleven or twelve, but the following year, my dentist insisted that this treatment had to be repeated every year. We just could not afford to do that, so he drilled and filled five of my molars. All were filled with amalgam – that's all they had in those days.

My teeth, themselves, were always good, but I have always had a mild case of gingivitis. The prescribed treatment by my questionable dentist was aggressive brushing of the gums, which is no longer recommended. My new dentist ordered a bacterial DNA test to check for any of a number of pathogenic bacteria that are typically responsible for gingivitis. None found. I was also tested for a genetic predisposition for gingivitis. Also negative. So that remains a mystery. Although, with vigilance, the condition has been improving. My wisdom teeth never came in, and an x-ray showed that all four were impacted and growing forward under the roots of the teeth in front of them. So in 1988, I had them surgically removed. And as for my throat, there's not too much to say except that I had strep about as often as I had pink eye. Another childhood memory... the ubiquitous thick pink medicine in the fridge that I would venture to say everybody has memories of – erythromycin. I actually liked it. I always thought that it was like a strawberry milkshake!

Continuing our journey south... heart and lungs. I have had no lung issues at all besides maybe a couple of chest colds.

Not so with my heart, though (and along with the heart, I include the entire circulatory system). First, throughout my childhood and beyond I was repeatedly told that I had what they used to refer to as "borderline" high blood pressure – it was usually low-130s systolic, mid-80s diastolic. It was attributed to my being overweight, and no treatment was ever prescribed until 2003 when I saw a new family doctor, and he measured my blood pressure in the low-140s over the low-90s. He prescribed – and I began taking – losartan (Cozaar®), an ARB (or "angiotensin receptor blocker").

I believe my blood pressure may have only been temporarily elevated, though, due to "white coat syndrome". I say this because the medication almost immediately gave me frequent periods of dizziness and light-headedness when I was at rest. Taking it at bedtime instead of in the morning helped a bit for a while. But about two years later, when I left my corporate job, and my stress level had greatly subsided, I felt dizzy and as though I would pass out almost all the time, especially upon standing. I had also lost my employer-provided insurance, so I stopped seeing my doctor and took the liberty of stopping the losartan on my own. It was expensive, and I felt certain that I no longer needed it.

What was probably my most significant childhood heart issue was discovered after I repeatedly complained of pain in my sides and a funny feeling in my chest when I exerted myself, like in school gym class (just about the only exercise that I ever got as a child). My doctor initially wrote it off as "side stitches" ("exercise-related transient abdominal pain",

46

or "ETAP") and said that it was due to my being overweight. The nature and cause of "side stitches", by the way, are still a complete mystery to the medical profession. So that was not a very conclusive diagnosis. And as with the headaches, when I continued to complain, I was sent for further testing. This time, I went to the hospital for an EKG (the old "moving pens drawing on a paper strip" kind). I believe I was about nine or ten at the time. It is a positive memory for me because I was fascinated by the machine and the science behind it – wires connected to my chest reading signals from my heart! The EKG showed a minor case of PVCs (premature ventricular contractions). We were told that these were, you guessed it, also due to my being overweight. They were not the cause of the pains that I had (those actually <u>were</u> "side stitches"). We were told there was no treatment for PVCs and that they were completely benign and that I would just have to learn to ignore them. Being a young kid and easily distracted by and engrossed in my interests, ignoring them came pretty easily to me. But I never lost my awareness of or ability to recognize them, and I have had them ever since.

Many people suffer from PVCs, and while they can be quite unnerving and sometimes even uncomfortable, they are generally of no consequence if the sufferer's heart is healthy with no underlying conditions. They often feel like a pause (sometimes referred to as a "skipped beat") followed by a thud in the chest. This is true for the most common type, anyway... unifocal PVCs. PVCs of this type originate at one spot (ectopic site) on the ventricular wall and always have the same timing with respect to the normal beats that precede them and the same waveform on an EKG. A variant of unifocal PVCs is multiform PVCs, which also have consistent timing but are seen on an EKG as two or more different waveforms. This is because the signal is conducted from the same ectopic site but via a different pathway each time. In contrast to unifocal PVCs are multifocal PVCs. These will look like different waveforms on an EKG and can occur with different timings. These are just classifications that doctors use (there are others, but they are far less common and usually associated with some type of actual heart problem) and are of no consequence to the sufferer.

But let's get back to my medical history... the overall most significant heart-related event prior to my developing chronic atrial fibrillation in 2006 was a bout of what I now know was also a-fib that occurred 14 years earlier. I had spent the afternoon and evening at an all-you-can-eat (and drink) company outing. It was an outdoor barbecue with lots of different foods and an open bar. I got a ride to the event, so I helped myself to my share (and then some!) of both the food and drink. There were tables, but I was standing most of the night – significant because the stomach can expand to a greater capacity when you are standing. When I finally settled in for the two-hour car ride home, everything in my abdomen pushed up into my chest, and almost immediately my heart began jumping around irregularly. It lasted the entire ride home, but I guess it did not concern me too much because of the alcohol that I had consumed. And I suppose, because it really just felt like a whole bunch of PVCs, which I was already accustomed to having and ignoring. Looking back, it was a clear-cut case of "holiday heart" – a-fib that is brought on by the adverse effects that alcohol can have on the heart (stimulation, increased blood pressure, and dehydration leading to electrolyte imbalance) and/or by a distended stomach and intestines, which can both stimulate the autonomic nervous system and put pressure directly on the heart itself. Still, this does not happen to everyone, and it does not happen every time (it only ever happened to me just that one time). So in hindsight it would seem that I must have had some sort of predisposition for it even then.

And what is the circulatory system without blood? I have had many blood tests in my life... beginning in my childhood. One theme that has repeated throughout my life almost every time that I have had a blood test – dehydration and low potassium. I believe that dehydration is pretty common... it's hard to drink enough water without really making a concerted effort to do so. And I remember trying to eat a banana every day for a while for potassium, but in reality, it probably did not make much difference since the rest of my diet was still poor. If I could just get myself to eat the recommended daily amounts of fruits and vegetables! Cholesterol was another blood issue. Mine was first tested in 1997 – we got a complimentary finger-prick test of our total cholesterol while at work. It was unannounced, so we hadn't fasted, and mine was 190... considered very good back then. I had never thought much about it before, or after for that matter, but then my new doctor ordered a lipid panel in 2003. My total cholesterol came back as 210... borderline. He didn't prescribe any meds... just ordered another test for a year later. I had stopped seeing him before then (I was saving up to leave my job) and never had the test done.

Years before that, though, an 18-month long programming project spanning most of 2001 and 2002, which had me working most weekends and even longer than usual hours, was drawing to a close as I developed a strange abdominal pain. It was constant and gradually got worse over the next few months. When I finally saw blood in my stool in mid-2002, I decided that I should probably see a doctor. I didn't have a regular doctor at the time because the doctor that I had been seeing since I left my pediatrician had retired more than ten years earlier, so I went to a random, nearby doctor. I did not like him and, looking back, I do not think his examination or diagnosis were very competent or thorough. (By the way, this is not the new doctor that I saw in 2003 who I referred to in the last paragraph.) This doctor that I selected at random performed a fecal occult blood test ("FOBT"), which came out positive for blood. He pressed around on my abdomen and told me that if there was anything wrong, he would be able to "appreciate" it with his hands (which I thought was a strange choice of words). He felt nothing, and said the blood was probably from internal hemorrhoids, especially since my job of late entailed mostly sitting at a desk. It made sense to me at the time, so this was just one more health issue to be added to my "ignore" list.

Let me back up a bit and fill in the history of my intestinal issues. I was a colicky baby, or so I've been told, with frequent bowel problems. As I got older, I remember having "travel diarrhea", as I call it... I believe it was a result of the anxiety or excitement that I would feel whenever we prepared for or left for a trip or vacation. And believe me, my parents just loved it! It would happen other times, too, whenever I was nervous or excited. That's why when I got a bout of it in school in 1974, everyone assumed that I had anxiety over something that happened to me in school. But it didn't stop once I got home, and I quickly became very weak with a low-grade fever and no appetite. I spent all of my time either in the bathroom, in the hospital for tests, or sleeping. I missed 33 (mostly consecutive) days of school that year and gave what seemed like a hundred tubes of blood for testing. My white cell count was sky-high every time, a sign that I had some type of infection. Blood cultures did not turn up any bacteria, so there was no medication that I could be given for it. It must have been viral, but no one could identify it. They called it an "orphan virus". I guess I had a good immune system, though, because it eventually cleared up on its own just as quickly and mysteriously as it set in. And for a brief period following this illness – and for the first time (and only time) in my life – I was not overweight.

Fast-forward, again, to the new doctor in August 2003. I was sure to bring up my abdominal pains and intestinal history with him. Not only was the pain that started two years earlier – the one that I had seen the other doctor about –

still there, but I had also developed another similar pain up higher in the abdomen, and I could now feel several lumps in the area. This doctor did not give me a diagnosis... he sent me immediately for imaging. I had an abdominal ultrasound that showed (in order) my right kidney, liver and gall bladder, abdominal aorta, spleen, and left kidney. Everything appeared to be fine. Then I had a colonoscopy, which showed internal hemorrhoids, as the previous doctor had guessed, and one polyp in my colon. It was removed and found to be benign. Finally, I was sent for an esophagogastroduodeno-scopy (EGD) – just like a colonoscopy but of the throat, stomach, and upper small intestine (the duodenum). I was not surprised to hear that I had a hiatus hernia (a condition in which part of the stomach protrudes through the diaphragm) since both of my parents had them, too. I also had significant irritation and erosion of the lining of the lower esophagus and upper part of the stomach around the cardiac sphincter.

I say this was no surprise to me because I suffered from very bad heartburn in my teen years and through college... so bad that calcium carbonate antacids (Tums®) provided no relief. I often drank a magnesium/aluminum hydroxide antacid (Maalox®) straight from the bottle throughout the day. Actually, I did this almost every day. Fortunately, an esophageal biopsy taken during the EGD showed that I had not yet developed Barrett's esophagus, a condition in which the cells lining the esophagus change to resemble those lining the stomach (a dangerous pre-cancerous condition).

The treatment prescribed for my condition ("GERD", or "gastroesophageal reflux disease" – common in people with a hiatus hernia) was rabeprazole (Aciphex®), a proton pump inhibitor (PPI). It worked great but was very new and very expensive, even with my insurance coverage. Omeprazole (Prilosec®, another PPI) had just become available over-the-counter, and while it, too, was expensive, it was much cheaper than the prescription PPI, and it worked just as well for me. When the generic became available, I switched to that and have now been taking it every day for the last ten years with no problems and no need for any other antacids.

As we near the end of my medical history tour, the next stop is my bladder. On the day after Labor Day 1994, I developed a bladder infection. It started early in the day as a strange sensation down below before progressing, first, to a frequent urge to urinate and then later in the day to a worsening persistent burning sensation then pain and darker urine. It soon became evident that the change in color was blood – by that evening, my urine had become red and the pain, excruciating. I finally went to the ER around 1:00 a.m., and the preliminary diagnosis based solely on a visual inspection of my specimin... bladder infection. The ER doc gave me samples of Pyridium® (phenazopyridine) for the pain, which worked great in about 10-15 minutes, and a prescription for the powerful antibiotics trimethoprim and sulfamethoxazole (together as Bactrim®). They worked well, but on the tenth day of a ten-day course of treatment, a rash broke out on my palms and neck. So now I list "sulfa" as one of my allergies.

OK, end of the line... my inguinal hernia. It started, I believe, as a simple abdominal strain (also known as a "sports hernia") way back in college during some indeterminate heavy lifting, climbing, or general roughhousing. I never had it checked out, and I never got the weeks of rest that would have been necessary for it to heal. Walking up and down hills every day, to and from classes, repeatedly aggravated it. And there was always lifting and straining, both in college and after, either on the job or during recreational activities. For 25 years, I never really rested it, and it continued to worsen the entire time (this is only my theory, of course, since I never consulted a doctor). When it finally "popped" in the summer of 2010, I needed surgery. The procedure was laparoscopic and all but painless, and I was back to my normal life in about a week.

OK, wake up! That concludes the tour and completes the list of the major health related issues that I have had in my life before a-fib. Again, I have listed these because I believe they all may somehow tie with my a-fib experience, even if only in a small way. You may see some possible connections between some of these and the things that I mention in the next chapter and beyond. To be clear, I have of course also suffered from numerous miscellaneous musculo-skeletal injuries over the years (never any broken bones, though), and I have taken many other medications, supplements, and vitamins other than the prescription and over-the-counter medications that I have mentioned in this chapter. I will mention any that I believe are relevant as I go on.

My Medical History

MY MEDICAL HISTORY: A CHRONOLOGICAL SUMMARY

As a baby, I suffered from colic and other bowel problems. Over the next few years, I would get hives while on aspirin, leading doctors to believe that I was allergic to aspirin. My baby teeth came in crowded, and by the time I was three or four, I started getting pink eye and contact dermatitis to dust and dirt, and I was given antibiotic eye drops and steroid skin cream. By age five, my chocolate allergy was identified, my blood pressure rose into the "borderline high" range, and I began suffering from chronic headaches. The doctor thought they were from sinus problems, and I took acetaminophen for them because they thought I could not take aspirin. At age six, one of my lower incisors came out with no permanent tooth behind it, solving the crowding issue. A couple years later, I contracted an "orphan virus", missed more than a month of school, and lost a lot of weight. Headaches continued to get worse, so I saw an ENT at age nine and was diagnosed with sinus inflammation and congestion due to allergies. A head x-ray revealed an unrelated nasal polyp. I began taking chlorpheniramine and phenylpropanolamine. Around this same time, I began complaining about pain in my sides and a funny feeling in my chest under exertion. As my allergy symptoms got worse, I saw an allergist for testing – allergic to all pollens, house dust, and cats. I was given the option to get allergy shots but just continued taking oral meds. As the funny chest feelings persisted, I went for an EKG around age ten and was diagnosed with PVCs – told they were benign and to just ignore them. As my ten- and twelve-year molars came in, they had deep grooves that needed to be sealed and were crooked, but I never got braces. At age twelve, I began using antacid tablets and liquids regularly. The next year, five molars had to be drilled and filled because we did not get them resealed every year per the dentist's recommendation. At fifteen, I was diagnosed with myopia and had my last case of pink eye. At sixteen, I had a severe sinus blockage and received a prescription decongestant, after which I began taking pseudoephadrine regularly. I tried chocolate this year and found that my allergy had gone away. I developed an abdominal strain (sports hernia) at age eighteen, which I was never able to rest, so it continued to get worse. My allergies also worsened, so I switched to diphenhydramine and was also now drinking Maalox® right from the bottle for severe and constant heartburn. My vision degraded to the point where I had to get glasses by age twenty-one, and the next year, I had my impacted wisdom teeth surgically removed. At age twenty-six, I had and ignored a two-hour bout of what I would later know to be atrial fibrillation after a long day of eating, drinking, and sweating (also known as holiday heart). Two years later, I suffered from a severe bladder infection, for which I was prescribed Pyridium® and Bactrim®. On the last day of treatment, I had an allergic reaction to the sulfa. Age thirty-one, a surprise, non-fasting cholesterol test read 190. I developed strange and constant abdominal pains at age thirty-five and discovered blood in my stool the next year. The doctor found internal hemorrhoids but ordered no tests for the pain. I started taking ibuprofen at age thirty-seven when a new doctor OKed it for use with an aspirin allergy. My cholesterol now tested borderline, 210, and I started losartan for my blood pressure. A colonoscopy revealed a polyp, which was removed and found to be benign. An EGD found a hiatus hernia and GERD, but no Barrett's esophagus. I started taking omeprazole and got off the other antacids. Two years later, a major stressor was removed and I began feeling dizzy, so I stopped the losartan.

ENTER ARRHYTHMIA

Christmas Day, 2006: I got up earlier than usual on this day to wrap Christmas presents that would be going with me to my mother's house later in the day. It was a cold day, and my programmable setback thermostat had not yet turned on, so I knew that it would be quite a while until the house warmed up. I was also just getting over a cold at the time, and my sinuses were still very congested. What is good for warming you up *and* for relieving sinus congestion? Coffee, of course (caffeine is a vasoconstrictor). I had only just developed a slight predilection for coffee the year before during a crazy sleepless 22-hour overnight trip to Niagara Falls and back to pick up my new food truck. I drank it more or less out of necessity that time, but since then, I had also just spent the entire summer waking up with coffee during my restaurant renovation venture. At home, though, I had fired up the old coffee maker on only a few rare occasions. And this cold, congested morning was going to be one of them.

But I could tell that the coffee was not going to be enough for my sinuses. I decided it was time to try the new long-lasting stimulant-based nasal spray that I had recently purchased. My usual routine consisted of oral decongestants and antihistamines (which I cannot recall if I also took that day - my guess would be that I did), but since I had this spray and needed some extra relief, I gave it a try. The day progressed as expected - family gathering at my mother's house before helping to prepare and then subsequently eating a big Christmas dinner. Then off to a friend's house that evening to watch the big football game. This friend likes to cook, too... even more than I do. So he had quite a spread of food laid out for us. And as a self-proclaimed bartender, he always has plenty of beer and mixed drinks at the ready. And even though I wasn't the least bit hungry, I ate and drank my fill while enjoying the game with my friends.

I got home from my long day of gluttony around midnight and sat down to watch some TV and hopefully digest some of the food that I had consumed that day before going to bed. As soon as I relaxed and reclined, the atrial fibrillation set in. I didn't know it by name yet, but I knew that it was exactly what I had experienced 14 years earlier under similar circumstances - the sensation of fish flopping inside my chest. I remembered that, when I had it before, I was sitting in a car, and when I got out of the car and stood up, it stopped. So I immediately got up out of my chair. It didn't stop. Well, I wasn't too concerned - I also remembered that, when I had it in 1992, it lasted about two hours. So I figured that, since I survived it for two hours that time, I would not get concerned until it went for more than two hours. And when it stopped after only about 30 minutes, I was pretty happy... and relieved. With that one single bout, though, it immediately had its psychological hold on me... I was hesitant to sit down again. In fact, I remained standing and walked around my house for at least two more hours to allow my stomach to settle to a point where I did not feel so full. It was already controlling me, but it had been a long, exhausting day, so I still found it quite easy to fall asleep.

The next six days passed without incident until... New Year's Eve. The party was at the same friend's house. Again, there was ample food and drink. We ate, we drank. I stayed there very late until I was certain that I was able to drive home safely, and when I got home, I went to sleep. No problems yet. The next day was the family's New Year's Day meal, though. And I was still using the nasal spray along with the antihistamines and decongestants as I had that whole week. In hindsight, then, it is not surprising that I suffered another bout of a-fib later that night. It was a repeat of the same scenario... sitting down to relax and watch TV. The a-fib started, and I immediately got up from my chair. I walked around trying to make myself burp and hoping that my stomach full of food would settle, thinking that that might relieve some of the pressure causing the a-fib. In my mind, at that point, it was the pressure of my stomach against my heart that was causing the a-fib (which I still did not know by name). Eventually, it just stopped on its own – whether because of or in spite of everything I tried. And again, it lasted just about half an hour, maybe just a little longer.

I didn't consider these two bouts representative of any type of "pattern" since the circumstances surrounding both were similar and extraordinary. I really did not give it much thought at all... until it happened again about six days later, and this time on a "normal" day. Yes, I was probably still using the decongestants... that had been my way of life for many years. But besides that, there was no excess consumption of food or any "drink" that day. And then, I had a fourth episode in *another* 5-7 days. And then, a fifth after about the same amount of time. Each time, the bout of a-fib would last just a little longer. A pattern definitely was emerging, and my engineer's brain could not overlook it... nor make sense of it. I had no idea what the condition was to even be able to do any research on it. I had no information to work with, and that bothered me more than anything.

On the night of the last Saturday in January (actually, around 2:00 a.m.), I had another bout of a-fib. This was now once a week for six straight weeks. After well over an hour of flopping fish in my chest, it didn't seem like it was going to stop any time soon, and I was just plain exhausted from the whole ordeal. I had never signed up for health insurance after leaving my corporate job almost two years earlier, which, by the way, may have been why I hadn't sought any medical attention at all up to this point (well, that, and the fact that I am a typical male). I really did not want to go to the ER for this, but weighing the estimated monetary cost against the potential benefit of *surviving*, I figured that it would probably be worth the cost of an ER visit. (It would be almost two years until I'd learn that, in actuality, it was <u>not</u> worth it.)

A typical trip to the ER, as I am sure many of you know, could be the stuff entire books are written about in itself. So I will try to keep the long story as brief as possible. Once processed in the ER, I was put in a room directly across from a nurse's station. A tech or assistant of some kind started an IV while an EMT who was hanging around waiting for something to do hooked me up to the cardiac monitor. Someone came in to take a tube of blood for the obligatory "heart attack" enzyme test, a nurse brought in the 12-lead EKG and hooked me up. I actually felt completely fine (besides being sleep deprived), and it was apparent that everyone could sense it because they all hung out in my room talking to me... it was like they were all bored until I arrived. I'm here, let the party begin!

After a considerable while, the ER doctor came in to tell me that I did not have a heart attack. Um, I never thought that I did! His diagnosis was "atrial fibrillation" - a completely foreign term to me. Well, except "fibrillation"... I knew ventricular fibrillation was bad. And I knew "atrium". Was this bad, too? He explained to me, in vague, broad terms, just what it was with minimal detail (or accuracy, as I would later learn), and he told me that it was completely harmless. He went on to say that there was no treatment for atrial fibrillation and that it would just be something that I would have to learn to live with. I cannot emphasize how unsettling this was to my engineering mindset, and I grilled the doctor about the cause of this strange disorder. He did not answer my questions very adeptly and kept mumbling about it probably being hereditary. So I asked him why, if I had indeed inherited it, did I not have it my whole life until now? Why did it just appear all of a sudden with no warning when I am forty years old? He said "Because you weren't forty your whole life," and then everyone had a good laugh. Remember, all the nurses, techs, and EMTs were still in my room. And they sure were enjoying the show. I think even the patients in the adjacent rooms were laughing. Ha, ha, ha.

Anyway, the doctor also told me that my blood test showed that I was considerably dehydrated and that my potassium was very low. Pretty standard for me. They hung a second bag of saline and gave it to me in a bolus by putting a blood pressure cuff around it and pumping it up. The fluid was cold and felt very weird going through my veins! I was also given a large cup of a salty-tasting, orange-flavored potassium drink and two giant potassium horse pills. Finally, they gave me a bolus and a drip of diltiazem (Cardizem®, a calcium channel blocker) in hopes that it would return my heart to normal sinus rhythm (NSR). And then we all just waited. Well, I waited... the rest of the crew floated in and out when the mood struck them.

Speaking of floating, all the while that I was in the ER, I had been trying to hold my urine because, being tied down with IVs and monitor leads, I wasn't sure how they were going to want me to go to the bathroom (I had never been admitted to the hospital or been in the ER long enough to know this). But with the bolus of saline and the large drink that they gave me (and the elevated heart rate making my kidneys work overtime) I *really* had to go. So I flagged down the nurse, and she gave me this little hand-held "urinal"... it looked like a tiny pitcher with a lid. It went up to 1000ml, but it just looked way too small to me. So with minimal privacy offered by the partially drawn curtain in my glass-walled fish tank of a room, I had to figure out how best to use this thing while still lying in bed. I guess it shouldn't normally be a problem, but I had held it for so long that I estimated that it would probably overflow if I tried to use it at too much of an angle. Somehow I managed, though. The final tally? Almost 950ml! That is twice what the human bladder is supposed to hold. When the nurse came back in to "collect" it, my natural reaction was to apologize... it just seemed so demeaning for me to summon someone to dispose of my wastes for me. All she had to say was, "Wow, you really *did* to have to go!"

I know what you are thinking, and you're right... I could have left that last paragraph out. But I felt that the story needed some comic relief. And my life (as I remember it, anyway) is full of comic relief, so I figured that the story should reflect it. But getting back to the a-fib, it did finally stop about an hour after the diltiazem was administered. Was it the drug? Was it the potassium? Or was it the water? Or none of the above? Who knows! I was already starting to get why this strange thing called "a-fib" is so difficult to treat – there's almost no way to know what causes it. But as I would later learn, managing dehydration and electrolytes can play an important role in controlling the individual bouts even if these things are not, technically, the "cause" of the chronic condition. To this end, the doctor had a nutritionist come in to discuss my diet with me. I told her that I do not eat on a regular schedule, that I never eat breakfast, and that I sometimes only eat one meal in a day. She told me that that was absolutely not acceptable and said that I *must* eat three full meals every day and drink at least eight cups of water every day (I think I was already drinking at least that much, though, so why was I always dehydrated?).

The doctor came back shortly before releasing me around 8:00 a.m. and told me that I should avoid the decongestants that I had been using, as well as caffeine, alcohol, and nicotine and that I should get as much rest as possible, especially during any future bouts of a-fib. Avoiding caffeine would be easy for me since I had only recently started drinking coffee and even then only on rare occasions, and I didn't even really like it. Nicotine would be even easier since I was never a smoker (besides a very occasional cigar), although I was subjected to quite a bit of second-hand smoke during football season in the tree house man cave that my friends and I built. Speaking of the tree house, we did have a tendency to consume quite a bit of alcohol up there during football games, so that would have to stop or at least be curtailed (for me, anyway). Not really a problem... I'd done a lifetime of drinking in college. Decongestants, though, that would be difficult. I'd have to find an alternative because I did have pretty severe sinus problems that affected my ability to function at times.

But that was it, those were my instructions, and then I was discharged. I was not held until the on-call cardiologist could see me. I was not prescribed any medication or referred to a specialist. Just told to eat more and get lots of rest. I would notice, quite some time later, that my discharge paperwork did say that I should get an echocardiogram, but I didn't go for one at that time because I still did not have insurance. Instead, I just cut my work load back to a minimum so I could sit around and do nothing most of the time... those were my orders. I practically doubled my food intake, as instructed. And slowly but surely, I gained weight. Lots of weight. Over the next six months, my bouts of a-fib became longer and went from occurring roughly once a week to at least once a day, sometimes multiple bouts per day. I had to give up my food truck business later that year, and I started working as a freelance IT consultant because I could do a lot of the work from home... while resting!

It was during this period of rest that I began doing as much online research about a-fib as I could. I learned all about the heart in general and about other heart arrhythmias, too. I learned about treatments, as well – both drugs and procedures. And I read about several "tricks" that might help me shorten the length of my bouts. Among them was the Valsalva Maneuver, which was originally designed to keep one's ears clear while diving. A modified version of this procedure can lower pulmonary blood pressure and reduce heart rate, which sometimes terminates a bout of a-fib. Ironically, the Diving Reflex can also terminate a-fib, and is performed by submerging your face into a bowl of cold water. Carotid Massage can also successfully terminate bouts of a-fib. In fact, my grandfather suffered from a heart arrhythmia for nearly 78 years, and carotid massage as needed was his only treatment. I will leave it up to the reader to research each of these "tricks" on his/her own.

Some other things that I have found that can sometimes help, either through personal experience or by talking to others, are eating or drinking something very cold, lying down, standing up, exercise, coughing, and burping. Eating or drinking something cold can deliver a thermal "shock" to the left atrium, as it lies directly against the esophagus. Sometimes just the act of swallowing anything is enough. Coughing and burping also apply or relieve physical pressure on the heart and/or the nerves that connect to it. A change in postural position can also change the pressure that your internal organs place on the heart and nerves. And exercise increases adrenaline levels, which can chemically "shock" the heart. The success of each of these tricks may depend on the "type" of a-fib you have, or they may actually trigger a bout of a-fib instead of or in addition to terminating it.

The "types" of atrial fibrillation that I refer to are two general classifications that I found while doing my research – they are not types, at all, but more like descriptions of the behavior of the a-fib. They are "sympathetically mediated" (or "adrenergic", influenced by adrenaline) and "para-sympathetically mediated" (or "vagal", influenced by the vagus nerve). The distinction between the two has to do with which branch of the autonomic nervous system – the system that silently controls all the body's systems and functions – has the strongest influence over the a-fib (the enteric nervous system – also known as the body's "second brain" – does not come into play here, as it only mediates digestion and elimination and does not innervate the heart). Some doctors buy into the theory of these two types, some do not. Personally, I believe that this kind of classification can sometimes be made, but the two types are not necessarily mutually exclusive, and the distinction between the two may often be blurred. In any case, this distinction usually becomes moot as the a-fib worsens. But generally speaking, a-fib that is sympathetically mediated will often be triggered by anything that raises your adrenaline level – stress, exertion, etc. – whereas parasympathetically mediated a-fib will be triggered more by things that involve the vagus nerve – rest, digestion, etc. And the things that trigger one type are often the things that can terminate bouts of a-fib of the other type. My a-fib was parasympathetically mediated (at least in the beginning), so as I would eventually find out, resting made it worse, and exercising made it better.

Try as I might, though, with all this new-found knowledge and a shiny new bag of tricks, my a-fib continued to worsen. I had increasingly more bouts throughout the days with pronounced spikes at night and during bedtime. Despite this annoyance, though, I did somehow manage to function. My business grew to the point where I needed a better office than the spare bedroom that I had been using – I needed a space where I could easily meet with my clients. So I cleared out half of my attached two-car garage and converted it into an office. I began this project in December 2007, one year after my a-fib had started, and worked on it whenever I felt up to it. I finally finished the following March. All the while, though, the amount of solid sleep that I was getting continued to wane. I found myself taking naps during the day, something that I had never done before (at least not in almost 40 years!), but that just seemed to make the a-fib worse. I hardly went out with my friends anymore, either, because I just never really felt up to it, and I preferred to be at home if and when the next bout of a-fib struck.

That spring and most of the summer were just one boring month after another without anything of any interest to report. In August, though, I really wanted to put forth an effort to help my buddies get our tree house ready for the upcoming football season. We had built this place two years earlier and gathered there religiously for just about every football game and a smattering of other sporting events. I wanted to uphold my part of our "tradition", and I really enjoyed the physical labor aspect of keeping the place in shape from one year to the next. But when I got there, I hate to admit it, I was not much help at all. The tree house lies more than 500 feet up a considerably steep hill, through thick fields of grass and within a wooded area on my friend's property, and I really felt like I could barely make the trip up there. It was very embarrassing for me because I am normally the type of person who jumps right in when something needs to be done, and I don't want to stop until the job is finished.

Meanwhile, my friend's wife, who is a cardiac nurse at one of the area's leading hospitals, had been repeatedly telling me (and her husband) that I should really see a cardiologist and get my heart checked out – that this a-fib might not be anything serious, but then again it might be! Either way, she said, there's probably something that can be done that would at least help a little. Of course, I didn't pay too much attention to her at the time. But I guess my friend did because, during a football game at the end of September, he had had enough of my "stupidity". I already hadn't shown up for a few games that season, and I wasn't feeling well at this particular one, either. He was visibly angry with me and ended up punching me (not a friendly punch) in an attempt top make me promise that I would see a cardiologist. I could see that he was seriously concerned, and that might have been the first time that anyone really showed serious concern for my condition. Well, for whatever reason, it hit home. It made me realize that I should probably be concerned, too. So I told him that I would do it.

I have always been a man of my word, and I have always tried to live a truthful and honorable life. It's now the next day, Monday morning. Yesterday, I told my friend that I would call a cardiologist... now I guess I have to call a cardiologist. So I looked up the only cardiologist that I knew of, called the office, and made an appointment. October 24th, almost a month away. I explained my condition to the scheduling person at the cardiology office, and she didn't seem to express any sense of urgency over it, so did I really even need to go? I really did not want to go, but I knew that I should. And later, I would be glad that I did. If anything, I should have gone sooner. If it wasn't for my friend's "tough love", however, I might not have ever seen a doctor about my a-fib. Or at least I would have waited even longer. Who knows where I would be now. So thanks for punching me!

But as the saying goes, and as is often true, there's no rest for the weary. On October 18th, less than a week before my scheduled appointment with the cardiologist, I had a bout of atrial flutter (which I had not yet known anything about) with a rate of about 190 beats per minute (bpm). I had never had such a rapid heart rate before, so I was a bit concerned about it (a-fib, by the way, does not really have a measurable actual rate since it is irregular, but sometimes the average rate can be fast and sometimes it can be slow). I waited almost two hours for it to return to normal, all the while trying to distract myself by watching TV and trying the same tricks that I had been using to try to stop my bouts of a-fib but with no success on either front.

So I made the trip to the ER yet again. This time they had a record of my a-fib from my prior visit as well as my medical history, so I was processed much quicker and then taken to a room. It was a little earlier in the evening than my first visit, and the staff seemed less bored. This time it was all business. I don't even remember the doctor who I saw, but an EKG confirmed that I had atrial flutter (another term for me to research). After a few shots of IV drugs, though, it eventually stopped (I believe it was diltiazem, again, and metoprolol, or "Lopressor®", a beta adrenergic receptor antagonist, or "beta blocker"). After I converted (returned to NSR), I was then transferred to a holding room of sorts to wait for the on-call cardiologist to make his rounds. I got no attention whatsoever from anyone while I was in this room. And it was so bright and noisy, I could not fall sleep. I was in for a long night of boring basic-cable television.

The on-call cardiologist arrived around 7:00 a.m. As it turned out, he was with the same cardiology group as the doctor that I had made the appointment with. I also recognized his name from an aunt who had seen him years earlier. That led to a few minutes of idle chatter, after which he verified my upcoming appointment with his colleague and then, seemingly independent of the ER staff, let me go with no medications, no discharge paperwork, and no instructions. If he had held me just a little longer, I may have got a "free" breakfast. Actually, I was glad that I was spared a meal that I surely would have felt obligated to eat. I thought that perhaps I still lucked out and might not be billed for this visit. Three months later, though, I would learn that I had no such luck on that front, either. But by then, saving money would be the very last thing on my mind.

The Doc, The Meds, and The Worsening A-fib

October 24, 2008... my first visit with a cardiologist. My first office visit with any doctor of any kind in almost five years. I was not anxious, though, because I was already kind of familiar with this doctor – I had met him briefly years earlier when he was treating a relative of mine for a heart attack. He was also the cardiologist on call who visited my mother in the ER when she had her first bout of a-fib almost one year prior. So I really didn't know anything about him, but I had a feel for his personality. At least he wasn't a <u>total</u> stranger.

When I arrived for my appointment with this new doctor, I was in NSR. I weighed in and was taken to an examination room where a tech performed a 12-lead EKG and checked my blood pressure. Then I waited. And waited. I was surprised that the waiting did not make me anxious as it often does, but the plethora of posters and heart models must have distracted me enough to keep me calm (I love visual aids!).

The doctor came in and listened to my heart and lungs, he sat down very casually and asked a few questions about my case, and then he just started telling me all about a-fib. It was much better and much different information than that which I had been given by the ER doctor almost two years earlier. Fortunately, I went into a bout of a-fib while we spoke (because, you know... I didn't want this guy to think that I was faking), and before I could even alert the doctor, he began to chuckle. When I did tell him, he said "I know. I can see your chest jumping around from here!" I told him that it would stop on its own in a few minutes, so he called the tech back in to do another quick EKG while the opportunity presented itself. His on-the-spot diagnosis: Plain old every-day a-fib. Confirmed. I felt a little better.

I still had the bulk of my 45 minute time slot with the cardiologist to fill, and big talker that I am, I had no problem filling it... and then some! When I told him about my ER experience and the very poor advice (in my opinion) that I had received from the staff there – to "get as much rest as possible" – he became visibly agitated. He told me that that was probably the worst advice that I could have been given and that there are generally no physical restrictions for lone a-fib patients, especially those who are largely asymptomatic as I was. In fact, he went on to tell me, exercise can often make the a-fib a better if it has not yet progressed too far.

Keep in mind, I was only 40 years old at the time with basically a clean health history, so the cardiologist's comments were made under the assumption that I had no underlying heart conditions (this a type of a-fib is known as "lone" or "primary" a-fib). To verify that my heart was sound, though, I would have to be run through a gamut of standard cardiac and a-fib related tests, as well as an allergy test for aspirin (he felt that everyone 40 and over should take a daily aspirin, regardless of a-fib, and regardless of any actual benefit that it may provide). I definitely wanted to be tested for everything, as I am a seeker of answers and of any kind of data that I can get my hands on. But at the same time, I dreaded it because I had lost my insurance after leaving my corporate job and, because of my clean health history, hadn't seen the need to purchase any on my own.

I was also not too thrilled to hear that he wanted to put me on medication. My dismay was mostly for the same monetary reason but also because I do not like having to be on medication – they all have side-effects, even if you are not aware of them. But with my blood pressure being mid-150s over mid-90s at that visit and with my history of borderline high blood pressure, the doctor thought it would be best to try to bring it down some. He told me that a lifetime of high (even "borderline high" – a classification that is no longer used) blood pressure was one possible cause of my a-fib, and it was important to treat it so the a-fib itself can be more successfully treated. Another possible cause, he went on to tell me, was sleep apnea. And that was especially a concern in my case since I was significantly overweight by then.

The doctor also discussed with me any other medications, vitamins, or supplements that I was currently taking. I told him about the omeprazole that I was taking for GERD. He said nothing about it at the time, but I later found out that PPIs such as omeprazole can deplete the body of magnesium and lead to arrhythmias. I also told him about the daily vitamins and the garlic and fish oil supplements that I took. He said the vitamins were OK. The garlic was also not a problem for him because it is the same as just eating lots of garlic, which may or may not have any health benefits. One specific thing he did want me to do was to triple my daily fish oil. He told me that any less than 1,200mg of DHA/EPA per day provides no health benefit. And for someone my size, more was better. So I started taking 6,000mg of fish oil per day (that's 1,800mg DHA/EPA). He told me that fish oil is not a "blood thinner", as some sources might suggest, but it does have a protective effect on the blood vessels, and it makes any clots that do form softer and less likely to break off and cause a heart attack or stroke.

So in addition to those instructions, I left his office that day with a prescription for lisinopril (an ACE, or "angiotensin converting enzyme", inhibitor), 5mg qd (once per day), and metoprolol succinate (the slow-release form of a beta adrenergic receptor antagonist, or "beta blocker"), 25mg qd. I also had an order in hand for a two blood tests – a lipid panel (recent findings indicate that high blood cholesterol levels can directly affect proteins in cell membranes, altering hormone receptors and blocking ion channels in blood vessels and in the heart, leading to heart arrhythmias) and TSH ("thyroid stimulating hormone" – most doctors will want to rule out hyperthyroidism as a possible cause of acute bouts of a-fib) and an order for an allergy test for aspirin. He also gave me a handful of clopidogrel samples (Plavix®, an anti-platelet agent that works similar to aspirin) to hold me over until I got the results of the allergy test.

I scheduled all the heart tests that the cardiologist wanted me to get at his group's private facility because they offered a 30% discount to self-paying patients, making it much cheaper than going to the hospital for these same tests. Besides the financial benefit, their facility was just a much more friendly and relaxing place than a hospital. So I first had the echocardiogram (or "echo", for short)... basically just like any other ultrasound but of the heart. The transducer is slid over the skin on the front and side of the left chest in different orientations. Quick and painless, but be aware that, if you are overweight, they may have to apply extra force to the transducer, which could be uncomfortable. The echo is used to measure the size of the heart's chambers and the volume of blood that they pump. It allows the valves and other structures of the heart to be visualized, too, so any defects in form or function can be identified, and it can show if there are major blockages of the coronary arteries, too.

The next test for me was the myocardial perfusion scan. This is a nuclear medicine test that involves the injection of a radioactive substance, Technetium 99m, in a process called SPECT, or "Single-Photon Emission Computed Tomography". (Be aware that each part of this two-part test currently exposes your body to the same amount of gamma radiation as about 500 x-rays.) Part one of the test establishes a "baseline" resting image of the heart. I received the injection, waited for about an hour (actually, I went out for lunch), and then, while sitting in a slowly-rotating chair with a gamma camera aimed at my chest for 20-30 minutes, a 3D image of the heart muscle emerged. This test was then repeated a few days later, but that time it was performed following a period of induced cardiac stress. They had me walk on an inclined treadmill for a few minutes to elevate my heart rate while administering a small amount of adenosine via IV. The image from part two is compared to that created in part one to determine if there are any areas of the heart that are not receiving proper blood flow, which would indicate a blockage or previously damaged tissue.

For me, the worst part of the myocardial perfusion scan was the effect of the adenosine. I had never had adenosine before, and I was unprepared for what it was about to do to me – it causes dilation of blood vessels throughout the body resulting in an intense all-over flushing, it causes transient AV block, which slows down your heart rate, and it causes bronchospasm, which gives you an asthma-like feeling (I imagine, anyway, as I have never had asthma). Put these all together, and you feel like you are going to pass out... at least, that's how I would describe it. The nurse administering the adenosine "coached" me through it, though, counting down the time remaining. I closed my eyes and just kept walking. Fortunately, adenosine has a very short metabolic half-life, so its effects end almost immediately after its administration is halted. The "passing out" feeling ends quickly, anyway. As I noted in my rear-view mirror, though, I was still a bit flushed when I went out for lunch afterwards.

The blood test was anything but exciting. Very anticlimactic, actually... waiting for almost an hour at the lab just to get called back to a small room where my information is verified and a vial or two of blood is drawn. I had flashbacks of my ordeal with the orphan virus in third grade. Was that the last time that I had had blood drawn prior to this? This test was a "lipid panel" (measures total cholesterol, HDL, and triglycerides), liver enzymes (to see if my liver was healthy enough to take cholesterol medication, should it be necessary) and TSH ("thyroid stimulating hormone" – a low result on this test could indicate hyperthyroidism, one possible cause of a-fib). And finally, the aspirin allergy test. I saw an allergist for this test, and it was a pin prick test very much like the ones that I had had as a kid. This time, though, there were only three drops on my arm – one with aspirin and one each of positive and negative controls. It took hours for anything to happen, during which I sat and read some magazines (not exactly my favorite pastime).

While I was running around trying to get all these tests done, I got a call from the cardiology office about my echo... it had showed a slight enlargement of my left atrium. This could have been the culprit of my a-fib, but it would be impossible to say for sure without a baseline echo from much earlier in my life to compare it to. So the enlargement could be congenital, or it could have been caused by my lifetime of elevated blood pressure, or it could have been caused by pulmonary hypertension, which, in turn, could be a result of sleep apnea... or any of a number of other things. Too many "could be"s! But it was enough to make my doctor want me to submit to a sleep study, and he wanted me to have it done before my next follow up appointment with him at the end of November. That was the whole reason for this phone call.

So in a few days, I was off to the sleep center. That was a very strange experience. First, I had to see a bariatric doctor in the same office (remember, I had gained 60 pounds from my a-fib at this point and was now well over 300 pounds). She would not directly recommend the low-carbohydrate diet that I wanted to go on (I wanted this because I had successfully lost over 60 pounds on it many years before), but she would admit that it was probably the best diet for weight loss. The only reason that she did not recommend it to her patients, she said, was because it was difficult to adhere to, and most people give up on it. Some people, maybe, but not me... I had done it before, and I would do it again. In which case, she prescribed a vitamin D supplement for me (I took an over-the-counter equivalent) because she said it would help with the weight loss. I started that diet about six years ago, and I am still following it today.

A few days later, I came back to the sleep center for the actual sleep study. It was strange to have an appointment at 10:00 p.m. – by that time I am usually winding down and getting ready for bed. On this night, though, I was packing a bag and getting ready to leave by around 9:30. I headed over to the dark parking lot after hours and went to the secret rear entrance of the dark building and rang the doorbell. It was very surreal. The person who let me in put me in a fancy hotel-like room where I watched TV until they were ready for me. The technician called me into his "workshop" where I sat in an uncomfortable, undersized chair in the middle of a large, white, sterile room. Very brightly lit and, again, very surreal. He glued several dozen electrodes to carefully measured points all over my scalp using a thick, foul-smelling glue, and when he was finished, he pulled a very tight knit cap over my head to hold them all in place. He strapped a microphone around my throat and motion sensors around my chest and abdomen, taped a pulse-ox sensor to my finger and placed EKG electrodes on my chest, arms, and legs. All I could think was "How the heck am I going to sleep like this?"

On a typical night, I flip over and roll around a lot in bed. Not this night. Because of the way the wires were routed and the location of the connector on the wall, I was forced to sleep on my left side. My left side had always been my side of choice for sleeping before the a-fib set in, but now lying on my left side made my a-fib worse. So worrying about that sure didn't help me to sleep that night. And just the fact that I was so restricted and in a strange bed in a hot room under the constant scrutiny of an unblinking night-vision camera... let's just say, it didn't go well. Still, I did somehow manage to fall asleep for a little while. An obnoxious wake up call shrieked over a speaker hidden somewhere in the room at about 6:00 a.m., and at that moment, I felt like I hadn't slept at all. Good thing I was self-employed at that time because I went straight to bed when I got home! OK, I washed the glue out of my hair first, but then I had to try to get at least a few hours of solid sleep before getting on with my day.

Just a few days after completing this battery of tests, it was time to head back to the cardiologist to go over all the results. They had already given me the results of the echo, and I learned that the sleep study, which was ordered because of the results of the echo, showed no apnea. That was good. I did have some hypopnea (shallow breathing), but my blood oxygen saturation level never dropped too low. My overall sleep pattern was classified as "abnormal", though... I certainly wasn't surprised! The myocardial perfusion scan came back negative on all counts, and the allergy test cleared me to take aspirin. So the doc stopped the clopidogrel and told me to start taking a 325mg aspirin daily.

Shortly after starting the metoprolol following my previous visit with my cardiologist, my a-fib had briefly stopped but then soon came back as my tolerance to the drug increased (A on Figure 1, page 250), so at this visit, he upped that dosage to 50mg qd (B on Figure 1, page 250) and ordered a Holter monitor (a wearable EKG recorder usually worn for 24 or 48 hours). My blood pressure was still on the high side, so he upped the lisinopril to 10mg qd. My cholesterol test showed borderline total cholesterol but "abysmal" (his word) HDL, or "high density lipoprotein" (known as "good cholesterol") – it was 31, and he wanted it to be at least 50. So he gave me some samples of Niaspan® (a prescription slow-release niacin) for the HDL and made me promise *not* to go to the ER for the flushing that it would certainly cause (apparently some people panic over this), and he ordered a follow-up lipid panel in three months to see how the Niaspan® was working. Oh, and my TSH level came back within normal range, so it was probably safe to take my thyroid out of the a-fib equation for now.

Before I left his office, my cardiologist stressed to me that it was clear to him that my heart was normal and healthy and that I **did not** have a heart problem but rather an electrical problem of the heart. He went on to assure me that my bouts of a-fib were <u>not</u> emergencies, so I should *not* go to the ER when they strike. Worst case, if I felt like I needed help, he wanted me to call their cardiology office – or their on-call doctor if it was after hours – first. He said that the ER staff is trained to save lives and life-saving procedures are generally uncalled for when treating cases of chronic lone a-fib. And especially since I was a self-pay, he did not want me wasting more money on another unnecessary ER visit.

By this time, though, I had already shelled out many thousands of dollars for doctors, testing, and medications, and it was evident that I was going to need to have insurance to cover the ongoing costs to support this unwelcome visitor nicknamed "a-fib". Unfortunately, the only insurance policy that I could find that would give me any coverage at all had a "pre-existing condition" clause, and it would only pay claims relating to that pre-existing condition after the policy was in effect for one full year. I did the math and figured that a year of premiums would still be cheaper in the long run than the potential lifetime of specialists, testing, and treatments that I might need. So I bit the bullet and dug into my savings and mentally prepared for the year ahead.

The costs were already starting to mount. At my January follow-up, my metoprolol was increased again to 100mg qd (C *on Figure 1, page 250*). Every time my metoprolol dosage was increased, by the way, my heart rate dipped way down, sometimes into the 40s, and when I asked my cardiologist how low was too low, he said "zero" and laughed. Then he told me that, as long as I felt OK, I didn't need to worry about it. So I didn't... it always went back up after a few weeks as my body got used to the new dosage. He also explained that it is more important to make sure that your "pulse pressure" does not drop too low – pulse pressure is the difference between your measured systolic and diastolic pressures, and it should always be at least 25% (one quarter) of systolic pressure. Another important concept regarding blood pressure is "mean arterial pressure" ("MAP"). The calculation of actual MAP is very complex, but for someone in NSR at "normal" heart rates, a good estimate is diastolic pressure plus one-third of pulse pressure. A result between 70 and 110 is considered normal, and under 60 is dangerous. If heart rate is significantly elevated, though, the formula changes and at very high rates is closer to just the actual average of the systolic and diastolic pressures. MAP cannot be accurately calculated for an irregular heart rhythm.

Anyway, also in January... the doctor had ordered another 24-hour Holter monitor before my next visit. It is very hard to go about your day as usual with irritating pads glued all over your chest, wires hanging down from under your shirt that get caught on everything as you walk by, and the bulky recording device clipped to your belt, getting in the way whenever you sit in a chair (especially a chair with arms) or try to wear a seatbelt. Sleeping with the thing is even worse... nearly impossible, actually! But I got through it (it was only 24 hours). I know that I had some a-fib and some PVCs while wearing it. We'll see if it picked them up.

In February, I received an order for a follow-up lipid panel and liver enzyme test to be done one week before my next appointment. When I eventually got around to calling in to make this appointment, they couldn't get me in until the end of March. So I went to the lab for the tests the week before the appointment and was hopeful that the prescription niacin (plus the garlic oil that I was already taking and a red yeast rice supplement that I decided to try with the doctor's consent) have done the trick. Anything to avoid more medications and more expenses.

But before I even made it to that follow-up appointment, I had my first bout of atrial flutter (D *on Figure 1, page 250*). It was a fast and regular rhythm, and I was completely asymptomatic, but it was something new to me, and I was a bit concerned. When it did not stop after two hours, I took an extra half-dose of metoprolol and waited for two more hours (a "trick" that my cardiologist told me to try for long bouts of a-fib). All the while, I tried to watch some TV to keep my mind off of it, but I couldn't really focus on what was going on in my program. So I figured "what's the point?" I must admit that I ignored my doctor's instructions to call their office first – it was 11:00 at night, and I didn't want to bother anyone. I just went ahead and made the three-minute drive to the ER. After all, now I had insurance to cover it!

If one thing has been consistent throughout my life, it has been my luck in these kinds of situations. It's kind of like waiting in a slow checkout line and then, when you finally decide to switch to a line that looks faster, that line slows down, too. Well, sort of. While I was waiting to check in at the desk in the ER, my heart went back to normal! I could have just left, I guess, but everyone had already seen me standing there, and I would have felt stupid to just leave. So I waited. And when it was my turn and I told them what happened, they took me straight back to a small side room – a non-triage room – for a quick EKG. All was well, so they let me go (yes, I did get billed for that visit, by the way). But while I was there, I talked for a bit with the nurse and learned about something referred to as "holiday heart", an acute form of a-fib... she told me about when her husband got it during a summer picnic. The light bulb went on, and I realized that that was probably what I had back in '92!

A couple of weeks later, I had my next follow up with the cardiologist. That's when he told me that the Holter monitor caught a few bouts of a-fib, as I had expected, as well as some PVCs, also expected. My HDL and cholesterol had both improved, but not enough (and though I had never had a problem with my triglycerides, they were even lower now). So I was rewarded with two more prescriptions... pravastatin (Pravachol®), 20 mg qd (he chose this cholesterol medication because a generic equivalent was available), and Niaspan®, 1500mg qd. My blood pressure was still elevated, so he upped the lisinopril to the maximum dose of 40mg qd. And because of the progression of my a-fib and the new appearance of a-flutter, he started me on digoxin, 0.25mg qd (E *on Figure 1, page 250*). This is the point at which he first broached the subject of ablation as a possible treatment. Yikes! I had never had surgery before and shuddered to even think about it. He recommended a particular electrophysiologist ("EP") at the University of Pennsylvania ("U of Penn" or just "Penn") who specialized in this procedure.

So off to the pharmacy I went, feeling like an invalid, reject, or otherwise sub-human... on five prescription medications now when only five months earlier I was taking none at all. I think that this fact may have had a greater psychological effect on me than the a-fib itself did. (But little did I know, the a-fib and flutter were poised to get much worse.) I filled all of my prescriptions except the Niaspan, which was very expensive and not covered by my insurance. Fortunately, my doctor had cleared me to substitute an over-the-counter slow-release niacin for it. NOTE: There are three different chemicals that are sold under the guise of "niacin" (or "vitamin B₃"). These are nicotinic acid, niacinamide (or nicotinamide), and inositol hexanicotinate (this one often marketed as "flush free" or "no-flush" niacin). While all of these substances express the same vitamin activity within the body, only **nicotinic acid** has the lipid-modifying effect for which niacin is often prescribed. Always read the labels!

Back at home, I began my exciting new life as a pill-popper. But within just a few days of starting digoxin, once touted as the wonder drug for the heart, my a-fib became much worse. The bouts were growing longer and more frequent... going from just a few times a week to every single day like the flip of a switch. So I started to do lots of research online. I even signed up on a website that allows users to enter a list drugs, vitamins, and supplements that they take, and it warns of any possible interactions as well as recalls and other dangers that may be reported. I had never been paranoid about this kind of thing before, but it seemed like there must have been some connection between my worsening condition and the new regimen of medications that I was on. I really hated the person that this a-fib was turning me into.

One of the most interesting pieces of information that I found at this time was that digoxin (and the natural form, "digitoxin", or digitalis toxin) is contraindicated for atrial fibrillation and that it may make a-fib worse and may cause other arrhythmias! Was it just a coincidence that my a-fib, which seemed relatively well-controlled by metoprolol, ran rampant once I began taking digoxin? I didn't think so. And the atrial flutter, which I only had on one occasion before, now came and went just as often as the a-fib did after starting the digoxin. So at my next follow up with my cardiologist at the end of June, I showed him my data, how my arrhythmias had gotten worse even with the additional meds. I told him what I read about digoxin, but he assured me that it was a safe drug and that it had been used for many years. He told me that the increase in duration and frequency of my bouts of a-fib were just the natural progression due to remodeling of the heart. I understand that this *can* happen... over time. Not in just a matter of days. The timing of it with the start of the digoxin was, to me, unlikely to be mere coincidence. I think at this point my case was pushing the boundaries of this doctor's expertise... he didn't adjust any of my medications during this visit and basically just insisted that my next visit be with the EP at Penn who he had recommended at my earlier visit. So while checking out, I made an appointment to see the EP.

Then luck would finally turn in my favor. Just about a week later, my cardiology office called to tell me that the EP from Penn – the same guy that I was planning on seeing (who, I found out later, had conducted hundreds of clinical trials of the pulmonary vein isolation, or PVI, ablation for a-fib) was leaving Penn along with two of his EP colleagues, moving to my area, and joining my cardiology group. Talk about an emotional roller coaster! Now I was happy. Happy that I wouldn't have to make one-hour-plus trips into Philly just to see a doctor... and thrilled that my cardiology practice would now have, not one, but three of the only 1,600 EPs in the entire country. It had to be a sign. A good sign! So I re-scheduled, of course, so I could see him right here ASAP.

Meet the EP

It was the second week in July 2009 when I went to see this new kind of doctor, an electrophysiologist, for the first time (F *on Figure 1, page 250*). My a-fib was still about the same... best described as "bad". I knew nothing about this doctor, so I was a bit apprehensive. I had hoped that I'd be in a-fib for my visit so he could see it first hand. And I was. Which was also good because it demonstrated to him that I did not have "silent" a-fib – atrial fibrillation that the sufferer is unaware of (which, based on my own personal experience, I cannot even imagine). I had a good rapport with this EP right from the start, and he seemed very willing to answer my questions and explain anything to me that I did not fully understand.

I must say that this first visit with an electrophysiologist was worth every penny. I left with a much better, more technical description of a-fib, how and where it happens in the heart, how the different medications used to treat it work, and the theory behind the surgical options such as ablation. I was sure to use the entire alloted 45 minute appointment, during which I unleashed my inner geeky engineer, whipping out the tables, charts, and graphs of the data I had collected. I was quite proud of these works and must admit that I was a bit miffed when the doctor barely acknowledged them except to say that it was just the natural progression of a-fib. I put a lot of work into these! Was he just "toeing the company line" now? In retrospect, I'd say probably not. I think that what he said to me was just the simple truth of the matter in many cases. The "hows" and "whys" often have no impact on the course of treatment prescribed.

But since we began gabbing as soon as he walked through the door, I really hadn't given him a chance to review my file. As soon as I got around to broaching the subject of digoxin, though, and voiced my concerns about taking it for a-fib, he glanced at my file. (Remember, he was new to this practice, and I am sure that he was not yet familiar with the preferences and proclivities of his colleagues.) I knew that he was looking at the right page in my file when the cold gaze of horror, disgust, and anger briefly crossed his face. He composed himself quickly, though, and proceeded to tell me that this (the digoxin) was <u>absolutely</u> the *wrong* treatment for a-fib. He went on to say that a lot of "old time" doctors fall back on it (mostly out of habit) because it is a drug that has been around for so long, but recent studies had showed that it was *not* effective against a-fib and can actually sometimes make a-fib *worse*. Ding! The funny thing is that the doctor who prescribed it to me was not an "old time" doctor... he was about the same age as my EP, and they were both just a few years younger than me! An old soul, maybe?

So he agreed with me on the digoxin... that's one more gold star by his name in my book. Another thing that I liked about this EP was that he told me that I was much too young to be on so many meds. My thoughts exactly! He went on to say that his preferred treatment of lone atrial fibrillation in healthy patients was an ablation, specifically the pulmonary vein isolation (or "PVI"). He explained that the ablation for right atrial flutter can be performed at the same time because it is done in the right atrium, "on the way" to the left atrium for the PVI. He had already done extensive work with both of these procedures and had overwhelmingly positive outcomes. Well, that was some good news!

The bad news was that my insurance carrier needed to see one full year of failed treatment with drugs before approving any surgical treatment options. My EP wanted to avoid prescribing antiarrhythmic drugs for me as long as possible because of the adverse side effects that they can often have, especially because I was not particularly symptomatic with my a-fib. To satisfy my insurance carrier's "one year of failed drugs" requirement, I would have to wait until at least November to have an ablation, but in light of the holidays, we thought it would be best to shoot for early 2010 instead. In the mean time, my EP doubled my metoprolol dosage yet again to 100mg bid (twice per day), and he also switched it from the succinate form to tartrate so my insurance would cover it. This is a very high dosage that I was sure I would just build a tolerance to again. The biggest problem with that comes when I eventually (hopefully!) try to get off of this medication. You must slowly wean off of beta blockers because of the tendency for the body to build a tolerance to them. Otherwise, the high levels of adrenaline that your body produces as a result of this tolerance can have a devastating effect if the protection of the beta blocker is removed too quickly. So... one more thing to worry about.

When I checked out after this appointment, the person responsible for scheduling time in the EP lab (where ablations and other catheter procedures are performed) checked the schedule for the beginning of the year. The third week in February was available, so I booked it. I felt both nervous and relieved at the same time, but I definitely felt like I was doing the right thing for me, which is a lot more than I can say for many of the other times that I have blindly followed doctors' orders throughout my life. Now, to just survive for seven more months. "Will he make it?"

Seven months with no scheduled doctor appointments... seemed strange. I only had a Holter monitor scheduled for the week before the ablation. That's it. So there was plenty of time for me to read up on the PVI and right atrial flutter ablations – I had to know exactly what I was in for. During this time, the frequency of my a-fib bouts did temporarily decrease, probably as a result of my EP doubling my metoprolol dosage and stopping the digoxin. But the damage was done, and it wasn't long before my tolerance to the drug increased, yet again, and the a-fib was back to it's "normal" level – about 10 to 12 hours of combined a-fib and flutter per day, every day. I wasn't terribly symptomatic (besides various side-effects from the metoprolol), but in this condition, I just felt better staying close to home (which was also close to the hospital) whenever I was in a-fib "just in case". Even though I had suffered from it for almost three years at this point, I still hadn't got used to the recently increased severity. Remember, only four months prior, my bouts averaged a total of just roughly an hour per day.

For the next four months, I made the best of "my new lot in life", trying to bide my time until my ablation in February when suddenly the a-fib and flutter got much worse – continuous, non-stop, all day long. It had never been this bad before, but I let it go for a day and a half and then called my EP. He sent a prescription to my pharmacy for flecainide in order to attempt a chemo-cardioversion – a single large (300mg) dose intended to chemically shock the heart back to normal rhythm. I went and picked up the flecainide and took 300mg, and I waited... and waited (G on Figure 1, page 250). Nothing. I called my EP back the following morning, and he told me that I could retry the flecainide after eight hours. So I did, and again, nothing. For a while there, I was taking 300mg of flecainide "tid" (three times per day, or every eight hours)... I had never heard of anyone taking anywhere near this dosage. Even so, it seemed to have no effect at all. After five days, though, the a-fib and flutter stopped as suddenly as it started, and for two full days, glorious NSR! By then, it had been over two months since I had two days of NSR. I stopped the massive doses of flecainide as soon as the a-fib stopped, but after those two days of NSR, the a-fib and flutter came back with a vengeance. I started taking the high-dose flecainide again, but after only two more days of taking it, I began to notice some adverse cognitive side-effects – confusion, difficulty concentrating, and inability to make simple decisions. It's hard to described, but I had never experienced anything like it before. To me, these were far worse than any physical side-effects that I could imagine.

I didn't want to, but I had to bother my EP again. He switched me over to propafenone, another antiarrhythmic drug. He wanted me to try a single 450mg dose as another attempt at cardioversion like before. And once again, it did not work (H *on Figure 1, page 250*). It did seem to make my flutter "permanent", though, keeping it from degenerating back into a-fib. I kept taking the massive 450mg dose of propafenone every eight hours just as I did with the flecainide. It never did return me to NSR, but it did succeed at keeping my heart rate down to about 120 beats per minute. Not a huge benefit, but I felt more comfortable at that rate than at 145, where it would have been otherwise.

The propafenone also gave me a bad metallic taste in my mouth, made my ears ring, and made me see orange halos around bright objects. I put up with these for one week before calling my EP... again. He ordered another 24-hour Holter monitor, which showed 100% flutter (with the ever-present PVCs scattered about throughout the day). Now it is just before Thanksgiving, not a convenient time to get the medical attention that I needed. So my EP told me to just continue taking the high dosage of propafenone until December 10th, at which time I should report to the hospital for an electro-cardioversion (a high-voltage electric shock delivered through the chest by a defibrillator that stops the heart, allowing it to naturally restart itself, hopefully in sinus rhythm) with a TEE, or "trans-esophageal echo-cardiogram" (an echo performed on the back of the heart by inserting a probe into the esophagus – used to check for clots in the LAA prior to a cardioversion). OK. Two more items to put on my list of things to be researched.

Perhaps as another cruel cosmic joke, though, the flutter stopped completely on December 6th, just four days prior to my scheduled cardioversion. The flutter stopped – I stopped the propafenone (I *on Figure 1, page 250*). NSR all day, every day, for the next three days. Another miracle! It seemed like it was over for good, so I called my EP, yet again... cardioversion was cancelled, of course. What purpose would it serve to shock a heart that's in normal rhythm? The very next day (December 10th, the day that I was originally scheduled to go in to the hospital for the cardioversion), the flutter and a-fib started back up in the wee hours of the morning (J *on Figure 1, page 250*). Ugh! So I started the propafenone again. The a-fib continued for five more days, averaging about 18 hours each day, and then it stopped again. After one full day of NSR, I stopped the propafenone again, and the flutter started up the next day. See a pattern here? It was the 17th, and for the last time, I restarted the propafenone. But after a few more days with no success, I called my EP... yet again. He had to be getting tired of hearing from me by this time. But he still took my calls.

But now my EP was preparing to leave for his holiday vacation and would not be returning until January. He told me to just stay on the high-dose propafenone for the next three weeks because, at least, it was helping to control the rate of my atrial flutter. He went ahead and scheduled me for another TEE/cardioversion in the hospital for January 7th. He also called in a prescription for warfarin with dosing instructions for me to follow on the three days leading up to the cardioversion. The purpose of the warfarin was to protect me from clots during the three to four week period following the cardioversion. The data clearly shows that, during this period, clots are many times more likely to form inside the heart; therefore, the patient absolutely must be on anticoagulant therapy of some sort to minimize the stroke risk for a month following an electro-cardioversion.

My EP also called in a prescription for amiodarone, a powerful antiarrhythmic agent. He did explain, at that time, that amiodarone was highly toxic and that it could cause many side effects ranging from merely annoying to life-threatening, and it is for this reason that amiodarone is typically only given as a drug of last resort. He said that the only other drug that he might have tried on me, at this point, was sotalol. But he hesitated to prescribe sotalol because it can cause fatal heart arrhythmias, and it absolutely must be started under close cardiac monitoring in the hospital for the first three days. So amiodarone was the lesser of the two evils in this case, and since I would only need to be on it for a relatively short period, I would be unlikely to suffer any permanent side effects. But I would still need the amiodarone to keep my heart in NSR after the cardioversion. (Remember, the sole purpose of the shock is to stop the heart. It has no lasting effects that would cause the heart to remain in NSR... that is up to the medication that is given after the cardioversion.) So in my desperate attempt to get off the medications that I was already on, instead I end up needing <u>more</u> medications. Waaah! They would (or so I told myself) only be temporary.

But wait, the string of cosmic jokes has not ended yet. I took the prescribed doses of warfarin for three days and then reported to the hospital on the morning of January 7th, as scheduled... 9:00 a.m. I jumped through all the usual hospital hoops - answering the same questions about my medical history over and over again, first for hospital's cardiac care center, and then for my cardiology group, and finally, for the anesthesia team (I wish I had just had a copy of this book to give each of them!). I was taken to a prep room where I changed into a gown and was shaved, and then an IV was started. About two hours had passed by this time. After waiting in this prep room for who knows how much longer, I was wheeled into the procedure room across the hall. I use the term "room" in the loosest sense, as it was more like a closet. There were already four people crammed in there when I arrived, and the doctor, anesthesiologist, and anesthesiology nurse had yet to make their entrances. Imagining the view from out in the hall after my procedure was over – it would look something like the iconic circus clowns coming out of the VW Beetle!

Once the full complement of clowns... uh, medical staff was present, and even more verification questions were asked of me and mindlessly answered, the doctor looked through my file. His expression told me that he was not finding what he was looking for – it was my INR result (INR, or "international normalized ratio", is a measure of how long it takes a patient's blood to clot as compared to standard, untreated blood). It became apparent that I was supposed to stop by the "Coumadin® Clinic" on my way to the hospital to get an INR reading. I guess my EP, being unfamiliar with the ways of his new practice, hospital, what have you, forgot to tell me that I had to do this. Oops.

No big deal, right? The INR test is just a finger prick and then about a minute for the machine to spit out a reading. Wrong. That would be too efficient, so they do not do it that way in the hospital. No, it is much better to wait for a tech to arrive to draw a vial of blood, deliver it to the lab, and then wait for the lab to test the blood and send back its results. Time had now stood still for me. An eternity later – drum roll, please – the results were in... 1.3. Bonk! My INR had to be in "therapeutic range" (between 2.0 and 3.0) for it to be safe to perform the cardioversion. So I now had two options, according to the doctor performing the procedure – get an IV anticoagulant (heparin) and have the cardioversion right now but then be admitted for a three- to five-day hospital stay so I could continue the warfarin and be monitored until my INR came into in therapeutic range (at which point it would then be safe for me to go home), or go home now and take more warfarin and come back in five days. I opted for the latter, of course (it would be cheaper, and the food would be better!). I finally got out of there around 1:00 p.m., exhausted from a whole lot of doing nothing. But with a new warfarin dosing schedule in hand, I hoped for the best!

Fast forward to January 12th... I went back to the hospital and had to relive everything (K *on Figure 1, page 250*). It was like a recurring bad dream. Same prep room, same prep, same tiny procedure room. But this time it must have been "bring your kid to work day" because there was a teen boy in the room in addition to everyone else that was there before. No one seemed to pay any attention to him. Was he really there? It was very bizarre. He just stared at me the whole time as I lied there, half-naked, and everyone just sort of worked around him. At that moment, I knew how it felt to be a zoo animal! In retrospect, I guess it was possible that he might have been a nursing student observing the procedure, but he looked awfully young, and he was just in his street clothes with no ID badge that I could see. Who knows. It's very unlike me, but I never asked anyone about him (I must have been distracted), so I guess it will, forever, remain a mystery.

Anyway, this time I knew to stop by the clinic before coming in, and my INR read 2.7... clear for take-off! The procedure itself was a piece of cake. Peel 'n stick foil electrodes were affixed to my back and chest and wired to the "smart" defibrillator. Lying on my left side, the doctor placed the TEE probe guide into my mouth. The anesthesiology nurse administered the propofol (a hypnotic agent), and I was out cold almost instantly. When I woke up in the recovery area (I don't know how much later it was, but it didn't take very long), I felt great... finally back in NSR after almost 26 full days of arrhythmia! They held me for about half an hour to make sure that I was OK to walk, but then I was finally out of there! My only instructions: no driving for the rest of the day, and start amiodarone as soon as I get home (which I did, though somewhat reluctantly after reading the compendium of warnings and possible side effects that came with it).

The very next week, I got a surprise call from my cardiology office. There had been a cancellation – they could get me in for my ablation next week, January 26th... three weeks ahead of schedule. Did I want it? Of course I did! The sooner the better. Yes, I felt a little nervous, but I knew, even though the thought of a microwave probe cooking my heart muscle from the inside (see *Figure 2a, page 252*) was a bit scary, that the risks of this procedure were minimal and far outweighed the risks of remaining on antiarrhythmic medications for life. I was excited just to be making an attempt at a "cure", though I was well aware that a-fib could not be cured, per se. But the RF PVI ablation that I was about to undergo carries a theoretical 85% success rate based on the statistics of the various pathologies of a-fib (of course, as with any skill-dependent procedure, the practical success rate is much lower). My EP felt that, in my particular case, the chance of success *might* even be a little higher, though, due to my age and overall physical condition. So I was very hopeful.

The only preparation for the ablation is to take warfarin to get your INR into therapeutic range by the day of the procedure. Normally, warfarin is prescribed for the five days leading up to that day, but since I was already on warfarin and in therapeutic range following my recent cardioversion, I was good to go... I just kept doing what I had been. And a few short days later, I was packing my bag and getting ready to take my heart into the shop to have it worked on... from the inside! Under normal circumstances, just the thought of this would completely freak most people out, including me. But these were not normal circumstances. These were the proverbial desperate times. And, well... you know the saying.

Three years of a-fib and now flutter had stripped away the life that I had once known. I had put all of my interests and anything that I found joy in on hold while trying to figure out how to just survive. At that point, I honestly felt (in the sense that I had withdrawn from life, as I had known it) that I may as well have been dead. And since all fear, ultimately, stems from a fear of death, what was left for me to fear? Any anxiety that I might have felt was only over the chance that this procedure might *not* rid me of my long-standing chronic atrial fibrillation, the chance that I might not be able to return to a normal life. But that was in the way back of my mind. I was more excited to just get on with it and get it over with than anything else. Desperate measures... here I come!

ABLATION

Monday, January 25, 2010: My brother arrived at my house bright and early to drive me to the hospital. Our mother tagged along so she could see the inside of the recently-constructed Cardiac Care wing. Oh, and I guess to see me off, too! My cardiology office gave me a Cardiac Center patient parking pass, which granted us a space in the parking garage *relatively* close to the entrance of the modern (and seemingly out-of-place with the rest of the hospital) Cardiac Care Center. After the considerable hike to the hospital entrance and then an even longer trek down an elevated corridor overlooking an equally modern and notably vacant lobby, we had arrived... the vast and opulent Cardiac Care Center waiting room. After checking in at the front desk, we made camp in a comfortable, distal corner.

This was it... the point of no return. Any anxiety that I might have had up to this point had completely disappeared. I was totally calm, and in an attempt to ease my family's tension, I suppose, I initiated some idle chatter. But before long my name was called – I was directed to one of the less-than-private check-in stalls around the corner where my personal information was verified, and I was tagged like some sort of rare bird by an ornithologist with the supremely important patient identification bracelet that would (if it lived up to its intended purpose) ensure the completeness and accuracy of my treatment and care over the next three and a half days. Then, preliminaries done, I was sent back to the aptly-named waiting room. The waiting *is* the hardest part.

As I emerged from the stalls and headed back to my still-warm seat in the corner, I noticed that there were some new arrivals in the waiting room, and I couldn't help thinking about the whole process being pretty much just like an assembly line – in one door, have work performed on you, out another door, in the next door, etc. And then it was my turn to move on to the next workstation as a nurse appeared through a set of side doors and beckoned me. Drawn to her siren song, I was led just yards down the sterile hallway to the imaging lab for a cardiac CT – "computed tomography", a series of x-ray images that are compiled into a 3D map of the physical topography of the inside of the heart. This would be the map that my EP would use the next day to guide the catheters during the procedure. I was impressed by the high-tech appearance of the machine – I can still see it clearly, General Electric's LightSpeed VCT®. An amazing device that synchronizes with the heart's rhythm and can render a complete image in only five heartbeats... a matter of seconds!

There wasn't much prep... take shirt off, don gown, insert large-bore IV in left arm, stick EKG-type pads on chest. I was laid out, most unceremoniously, upon this humming wonder of modern technology that lie before me and fed into its gaping maw, feet first. CT machines, by the way, are really just like big donuts, not coffinesque tubes like MRI machines are. It wouldn't have mattered either way, though, as I was only inserted up to my chest. Then my IV was connected to an automated contrast agent injector, and the monitor wires were snapped onto the electrodes on my chest. The machine was completely automated and guided me through the whole process with its pleasant femtronic voice. "Please place your hands on the designated areas on the front of the machine", "Breathe normally", "Hold your breath", etc. It even did a trial run, first, to make sure that I did it right.

Then came the real thing – the various moving parts whir as they spin up to speed, contrast agent is injected, the x-ray beam switches on. The table moves about eight inches then... done. It was over in just a few seconds, but I had to remain in position for a few minutes while the computer generated the image... "just in case". And I knew what that meant – there'd be a problem. Yep! Something with the contrast agent. They checked the pump and asked me if I had any pain at the IV site. I guess they thought that maybe they missed the vein. But it was 500ml of contrast agent, so if it went in intramuscularly or subcutaneously, I certainly would have felt (and seen!) it. No time to investigate, though, as the lab had a schedule to keep. So they reloaded, and we did it again. Success! The worst part (actually, the only unpleasant part) was the intense warm, full feeling in the bladder that the contrast agent causes. I was warned about this side effect in advance, but it still caught me by surprise. No accidents, though... fortunately!

With the IV hole on my arm bandaged and a few less chest hairs, I rejoined my family back in the big fancy waiting room. Tick, tick, tick. My name was called again. This time, the siren was behind the reception desk. She told me that it was time to move on to the next stop in the assembly line – admissions. It was another long trek, a journey to one of the oldest buildings of the hospital complex. Gray block walls, gray floors, almost prison-like. Not modern or cheerful at all and quite the opposite of what we had become accustomed to in the Cardiac Care Center's waiting room, that's for sure. We were led to an undersized room with one bed against the wall and no chairs and were left there to wait some more. It was around this time that I was starting to mind the "no food after 7:00 a.m." part of my pre-admission instructions.

Several people flitted in and out of this little room just long enough to check my almighty wrist band and ask me to verify my information. I could hear them talking in the hall, too, which gave me zero confidence that anyone knew what I was doing there. A tech came in to draw blood, but no one seemed to know for what purpose. And when another nurse wheeled in a gigantic livestock scale a short while later and asked me to step on it, I had the sudden urge to moo! This would be the moment that my family first realized the true extent of the weight gain that I had suffered by following that ignorant (to put it nicely) ER doctor's instructions for the first two years following my initial diagnosis.

"139 kilograms" the nurse proclaimed as she recorded it on my chart. Thanks a lot, lady! My brother, a math tutor and human calculator, instantly looked shocked. My mother, not so much... what's a kilogram? It works out to about 307 pounds, in case you were stumped. A sixty-some-odd-pound gain over my pre-diagnosis weight of roughly 245 pounds. No wonder I was feeling lousy. By the way, that 245 pounds might still seem like an awful lot, but I am 6'1" tall and large-framed, and it is actually considerably less than my weight throughout all of high school. (That's the good thing about having always been overweight – I'm the only one in my circle of friends who weighs <u>less</u> than they did back then.)

The next embarrassing step in the process was the shaving. Yep, stem to stern. OK, shoulders to groins, actually. Front and back. Yay! If I were forced to pick a positive thing about this experience, I was glad that the nurse let me do it myself. But they wanted me to do it right then and right there. Well, in the bathroom... but with my family waiting (and listening) just outside the door. Oh well, did it, and it was done. A few minutes later (and a few pounds lighter!) a different nurse came in to start an IV. She noticed the bandage from the IV that I had earlier for the CT contrast agent. Angrily, she asked why they didn't just leave that one in for her to use. She said that it would have been so much better than the one that she would put in because it was a larger bore than what they normally use in admissions. How should I know why they took it out? Was I supposed to tell them to leave it in? She made it seem that way, but maybe she was just being rhetorical... and having a bad day, apparently. Oh well, just stick me again... it certainly would not be the last time I'd be stuck during this stay. That's for sure!

This new IV was for heparin, an anticoagulant derived from the lining of pig intestines. I was very nervous about getting heparin because I had heard horror stories of dosages being set wrong and patients bleeding to death. But two nurses came in to hang the bag, calculate the dosage, and set the meter – each verifying the work of the other. So I felt a little better. And ah... I could feel my blood thinning right away. Not really (anticoagulants do not actually "thin" the blood!), but I did wonder why I was getting heparin in addition to the warfarin that I had already been taking. Oh well, I figured the highly-paid medical professionals must know what they are doing (naïve, I know). It was now about 2:00 p.m., and my family wished me well and then left for home as I was about to be taken to my "overnight" room. I was just anxious to get it all over with. To be honest, the only thing that I really wanted was food. I was starving by this time, but I was still NPO ("nil per os" or "nothing by mouth") until after my TEE, which was scheduled for 3:45 that afternoon.

Just as a nurse came in to wheel me to my temporary room among the hospital's general population, I could hear a hurried gait approaching out in the hall. "Stop his heparin!" this second nurse cried, urgently. How did I know there was going to be a problem? The blood that was drawn when I first arrived in admissions was, apparently, to test my INR, and the heparin was only to be administered if my INR was too low. Maybe my file did not reflect that I had been on warfarin? Someone must have known, that's why the INR test was performed. No worries, though. I wasn't bleeding from my eyes, yet... or any place else that I could see. And to make sure that it stayed that way, the second nurse promptly hung a bag of vitamin K and set the meter for rapid induction... 15 minutes. By the time I was delivered to my new home for the night, the bag was empty. A vampire came in a while later for another vial, I assumed it was for another INR test, which (I also assume) turned out OK this time.

I tried to settle in to my new surroundings to watch a little TV, but I was on the verge of delirium from hunger by now. Before long, a transport minion arrived to wheel me back over to the cardiac wing for my TEE. Easy, right? Remember, I had had that TEE prior to my cardioversion, so I knew it was going to be the oft referred to "piece of cake". Or did I? Different doctors have different ways of doing things, as anyone under the care of multiple doctors can attest to. But I would still expect, at least, some level of consistency between identical procedures performed at the same facility. It shouldn't matter who performs the procedure. Ah, silly me! Whoever wrote the orders for my first TEE specified that propafol, a hypnotic agent that induces a complete and total loss of consciousness, be used – perfect for me! I didn't want to be the least bit aware or have any memory of it afterward.

But this time, as I would soon learn, the orders called for standard conscious sedation using a Versed® (midazolam, a benzodiazapine) and fentanyl (a synthetic opioid).

I already had the IV in my arm and was not getting a cardioversion after this TEE, so they did not need to do any additional prep this time around – I was taken directly to the tiny procedure room. There was only one other person there when I arrived. A nurse... a big, football-player-looking guy. Very friendly. I can almost remember his name. Joe? John? I must have been ahead of schedule because we just flapped the gums for a while (something that comes very natural to me in just about any situation). When I told him what I was there for (an ablation), he told me that he had been wanting to assist on one of the new PVI procedures and that it was a good week for him to try to switch his schedule around so he could assist with mine the next day. Hey, that sounded good to me... then I would at least sort of know someone when I got wheeled in there the next morning.

The phone rang, and the levity came to an abrupt end. It was the doctor who would be performing the TEE, and it was time for us to get down to business. The nurse gave me a lollipop... and, in his words, "not the good kind." Boy, was that an understatement! It was a glob of thick, slimy lidocaine gel, bearing the ubiquitous imitation cherry flavor of so many other medicines (that, in this case, was grossly outmatched by the bitterness of the medicine itself), smeared on the end of a wooden tongue depressor. I don't gag often, but this "lollipop" just about did me in. I was supposed to keep it in the back of my throat and swallow repeatedly. Why didn't I have to do this the last time that I was in for a TEE? Who knows... I just complied. I was way too hungry to fight and just wanted to hurry things along.

When the doctor finally graced us with his presence, we exchanged some brief gallows humor before he had me roll onto my left side, facing him, so he could spray an even fouler-tasting numbing spray into the back of my throat. Meanwhile, behind my back and unbeknownst to me, the nurse had injected the prescribed amounts of fentanyl and Versed® into my IV. The doctor poked me in the back of the throat with a tongue depressor, and I gagged. What did he expect? He looked at the nurse and asked if he had administered the sedative yet. The nurse replied in the affirmative. I'm guessing that I was supposed to be out, or almost out, by that time. So the doctor ordered more of each. Nothing. And then, a third dose of one... can't remember which. But now the maximum dose for both medications had been given, and I was still wide awake.

I honestly did not feel the least bit sleepy or even woozy. But hospital schedules must be adhered to, so the doctor said, "OK, here we go." He gave my throat one last coat with that delicious spray, put the guide between my teeth, and shoved the garden hose down my throat. I gagged and wretched like I never have before or since. To this day, that was the single most unpleasant experience of my entire life. And as one last bit of cruel cosmic irony, I actually did fall asleep right as I was being wheeled out and returned to my room. And when I awoke, my dinner had already been served. There it was, waiting for me... I could finally eat! It probably wasn't warm anymore, but at least this long, grueling day would end on a somewhat positive note. Food!

Guess again. My throat, chest, and abdomen were so sore from the violent ordeal that they had just been put through, that I could barely swallow. I only managed to sip some tepid broth and let less than half a can of warm soda trickle down my throat. Oh, and I ate maybe a spoonful or two of the gum-based non-gelatin dessert (aka sour yellow slime). It was better than nothing at all, I guess. Nutritionally speaking, anyway. But it sure was not the positive note that I was hoping for... I was still starving. And I didn't think I would be able to sleep at all that night because of the pain, but I guess I really was exhausted because I fell asleep long before I was ready to - right in the middle of one of my favorite TV shows. That was a good thing, though... less chance to think about what was to come tomorrow.

Tuesday, January 26th (L on *Figure 1, page 250*): It seemed as though I had only just fallen asleep when a nurse came in to wake me. It was 7:00 a.m. and time to get ready for surgery. I bathed and shaved (my face!) using the highly-perfumed toiletries (at least, they seemed that way to me, as I use mostly unscented or lightly-scented products - a carryover from my scent-free childhood - out of deference to my mother's sensitivity to fragrances) that were kindly provided by the hospital (I wonder how much I actually paid for them) because I knew that it would be the last time that I would be able to do these things for at least the next few days. I was NPO, again, so no breakfast allowed. I never thought that I could feel so hungry! And then, without warning, another black-shirted minion materialized by my bed to whisk me away, back to the cardiac care center again, my destination this time [cue dramatic music]... the EP Lab.

From my bed parked in the hall just outside of the EP Lab, I witnessed the flurry of activity all around me as everyone prepared for the big event. Remembering my own assembly line analogy from just the morning before, though, it struck me that this was probably just another day at the office for these people. I hope *they* got enough sleep! The doors of the lab opened, and it was like a geek's Taj Mahal inside (what little of it that I could see while lying flat on my back, anyway). A magnificent palace of technology, the focal point being an array of large, flat-panel displays hanging from above on a gimbaled mount that could be swung to just about anywhere in the room – the envy of any sports bar, for sure.

There were also racks upon racks of electronic equipment. Lights, knobs, buttons, and wires as far as the eye could see, but I could not fully appreciate it all from my mandatory supine pose. And with everyone stopping by to bother me with their introductions, I couldn't appreciate what I was seeing, anyway. Nurses, technicians, anesthesiology staff, the jester, knights, eunuchs, and miscellaneous onlookers and standers-by. There were about 15 people in the room, and I had forgotten to look for the nurse from my TEE the day before. But he was there... John! I was glad to see a familiar face. When I caught him up on my post-TEE condition, he apologized for it being so unpleasant for me. That struck me as funny because it certainly wasn't his fault!

Once we all knew each other, I was scooted off my bed and onto the workbench, which was about half the width of my generously-proportioned body. How would I not roll right off and onto the floor? The staff converged on me from all sides... that held me in place for the time being. What really impressed me was that everyone was so friendly. How was that possible so early in the morning? Then a comment that I might be the best-smelling patient that they had ever had, and I immediately credited the hospital-provided products. Didn't want them thinking that I always smelled like that! I guess they were just hinting that most patients smell worse. Dispensing with the pleasantries, though, they had me sit up so they could pull off the hospital's heart monitor pads and replace them with their own, apply sticky foil grounding pads to my back, chest, arms, and legs and soft silicone pressure-relief pads to my coccyx, heels, and elbows. They started two more IVs and put a pulse-ox sensor on my finger.

In this position, now sitting upright on the cold steel chopping block, I got a much better look around the room. I knew that I was going to be knocked out pretty soon, so I figured that I'd ask questions while I had the chance – lots of questions. I was curious about all the equipment and the technologies that would be used. Some of the less busy staff members had some questions for me, too, which got me talking about my a-fib history. I probably recited everything in the last three chapters to them, or at least I tried to. Eventually, I had to lie down again so they could position the side retaining rails that would keep my arms (and the rest of me!) from falling off the table once they all moved away. My EP floated in around this time, greeted me pleasantly, told me that everything looked good and should go smoothly, gave me and the equipment a once over, and then left (and not through the same door through which he entered, which struck me as odd... was this room a thoroughfare? Would others be passing through while I was unconscious and on display?). As it turned out, I wouldn't see my EP again until the next day – he didn't return to the lab until the rest of the prep was complete and I was unconscious.

The staff continued with their part after he left, doing their best to identify anything that I might find painful or uncomfortable so they could adjust or insert additional padding. I was going to be lying there in that one position for a very long time, so the more comfortable I was while I was awake, the less likely it would be that I would have severe pain afterward. That was the theory, anyway. And comfort is a relative thing, so when there was no more comfort to be had, their final step was to cover me up to make sure that I was warm enough. Again, this was temporary, too, because they'd have to uncover me to finish up the bulk of the prep work after I was knocked out.

Post knock-out prep included the immobilization of my right wrist and insertion the arterial line (a-line) into the right radial artery, which allows for real-time blood pressure monitoring during and after the procedure, insertion of a Foley catheter into my bladder (ouch, glad I was out for that one), insertion of a TEE probe into my esophagus (that wouldn't have felt too good, either, after what my esophagus went through the day before), and insertion of a breathing tube into my trachea. Maybe they did some other things, but this is all I could glean from the post-procedural state of my body. Finally, the catheter sheathes would be inserted into the femoral veins in both of my groins, at some point after which the EP would then make an appearance to do his part. While the procedure is actually performed, I would be completely covered by a tarp, as though I were not even there. This would keep the attention of the staff focused on the video displays in front of them and the surrounding electronic equipment. [sigh] OK, I'm ready... let's roll!

It was about 8:30 a.m. The anesthesiology nurse was about to put the mask over my face when I quickly asked her about the anesthesia. Her answer – the only word that I heard, anyway – "Propafol." Great! I did so well on that for my (first) TEE/cardioversion... no side effects at all. What I might have also heard but paid no attention to was something about gases. I know, now, that propafol is just used to initially knock you out while the endotracheal tube is inserted, and then the anesthesia gases that will completely paralyze the body are administered through that tube. Oh well, I guess having a false sense of security was better than having none at all. With that, the mask was secured around my nose and mouth. It was just oxygen (and a distraction). After a few deep breaths, everything got bright and buzzy as the O_2 bathed my brain cells, and before the nurse could even finish saying that she was starting the propafol, I was on my way to another dimension. I would have to watch the remainder of the procedure (someone else's, of course) online after I got home. And for the next nine hours, I would cease to exist... to my own mind, anyway.

It was an indeterminate amount of time later when consciousness slowly returned, accompanied by confusion. Actually, I didn't even recognize it as consciousness at all. It seemed like maybe I was hearing voices and other sounds, or maybe I was imagining them. Could I feel anything? I wasn't sure. But I couldn't move. Was I coming out of my anesthesia too soon, during the surgery? Or maybe I didn't even make it... how would I know? The best way to find out would be to open my eyes. I struggled with eyelids that felt like pork chops for what seemed like an hour before I could get them to move. And then, there was light. And with concerted conscious effort, my eyes began to focus. OK, it appeared that I was in a bed, in a room. A nurse at a desk outside. I felt a bit confused, but pretty confident that I wasn't imagining any of it and that I had made it through the procedure.

It was dark outside the window. I could see that. My post-anesthesia vision (even with my glasses, which someone had already placed back on my head) made it tough to even locate the clock on the wall. It was an "old fashioned" analog clock. Did it say 5:30? Could this procedure really have taken nine hours? Or was it morning, was it evening the next day, or later? Maybe days later! As I slowly regained sensation throughout my body, I started to think, based on how bad I felt, that anything was possible. I have never been hit by a truck, but at that moment, I was fairly certain that I now knew how it would feel. And for as hungry as I was going into this surgery (having not eaten for more than 24 hours), the last thing I want to do was eat. Of course, this would be the time that there was a tray full of food right next to me. I could sense the ethereal guffaws at my expense.

My lucidity had now risen to a level high enough for me to recall that I was supposed to be in the ICU following my procedure, and indeed, that's where I found myself. No, nothing had gone wrong, this was a matter of standard procedure for the PVI ablation (at this particular hospital, anyway). In the ICU, there is one nurse assigned to every two rooms. My nurse came in to see how I was doing and told me that I should try to eat (even though I was also instructed to remain lying flat on my back for the next 21 hours). Not only did I feel far too nauseated to even think about eating, but my throat was still extremely sore, even more so than it was the night before, and I couldn't eat then already. I have never more desperately wanted just to go back to sleep than at that moment. Just let me sleep until I feel better... can't you nourish me through my IV?! We all know that I could not get away with that, though. So I just picked and sipped on very small amounts of anything soft or liquid. Yes, it was helping to keep me alive, but more importantly it also kept the nurse off my back.

I hate to dwell on this fact, and maybe it is because I have (thankfully!) not been through much physical trauma in my life, but words truly cannot express how awful I felt. But I am pretty tough, and I went into it knowing, full well, that I was going to feel lousy for a while. I just hoped it would prove to be worth it in the end. I was quite weary from the events of past 24 hours, and just as a wise man had once noted, there really was no rest – instead, there were nurses coming in with pills for me to try to swallow and what seemed like a constant rotation of techs coming to either take blood, do an EKG, get a chest x-ray, or do an echo. Between all that and the IV pumps constantly beeping as bag after bag needed to be replaced (there was saline & dextrose, heparin, amiodarone, and an antibiotic), the Foley bag contents needing to be regularly drained, measured, and discarded, hourly groin inspections (of the puncture sites), and periodic electronic Doppler monitoring of plantar blood flow in each foot, sleep was but a dream that night.

Wednesday, January 27th: Even though I hadn't slept much, I felt so much better on this new day. It's all relative, I guess, because I still felt like I might have fallen off of a two-story building. I was able to eat a little more than the day before, and I slept a bit more comfortably off and on between interruptions (the same rotation of interruptions that I had been plagued by throughout the night). The worst part was that I still had to remain lying flat on my back until a full 24 hours had passed following the conclusion of my procedure. The worsening back pain was slowly overtaking any other discomforts, and one of the nurses, perhaps divining my agony from the incessant groans and the distressed look on my face, raised my knees, ever so slightly, with a wedge pillow to try to make me more comfortable. But that provided only slight relief, and it made the stabbing, burning pains in my heels more intense and noticeable.

My mother had called into the ICU sometime that afternoon to see how I was feeling, and I was surprised to learn that her and my brother had come back to the hospital during my procedure the day before. They arrived close to when they thought it was going to be over (I think I had given them some ridiculously short estimate), and they expected to be able to visit with me afterwards. She told me that they waited for at least three hours without hearing anything from anyone, but I don't know if anyone even knew that they were there waiting. When they had alerted one of the women at the desk that they were there and that they were waiting for me, she checked with the EP Lab and then told them that the procedure would be over soon and that the doctor would be out to see them when it was.

My mother told me that he (my EP) came out to talk to them around 3:30 that afternoon. So I could figure out about how long the procedure lasted – roughly seven hours from the time that I was knocked out until he finished up and could leave the lab. He told them that it went well but that I was still out of it and that I would be in recovery for two more hours. She told me that he seemed very nice and polite, but he looked sweaty and disheveled (no wonder, he was on his feet for at least seven hours wearing a 15-pound lead apron and performing a very serious, high-stress task). Since they had already been there for four or five hours by that time and were very hungry, they decided to leave and then call back later in the evening. She said that when she called, though, the nurse told her that I was asleep. Very doubtful. I am sure that I was *trying* to sleep, it might have even looked as though I was asleep, but no. Still, I am positive that I was in no condition to talk on the phone at that time, anyway.

The next thing that helped to break up the long, boring day after surgery – doing nothing but lying in bed watching boring daytime television – was a visit from the hospital's patient advocate. She asked me all sorts of questions about my comfort, my nurses, my doctors, medications I was taking, and my insurance company and coverage. I spoke frankly about everything, as I always do, and she explained that she was there to take care of any problems that I might have... *free of charge.* Armed with notes from our conversation, she went to a desk just outside my room and began making phone calls. I could hear her talking about things like my meals, drug substitutions, co-pays, and deductibles. She came back in and told me that she was waiting to get calls back from a few people, and that she would either be back to update me on anything that she was able to resolve, or I would get a letter in the mail from her office after I returned home. She never did come back, and I never got any letter. None of my complaints had been resolved, either, so I can't help but wonder if it was all just for show... you know, to earn the hospital a higher score on the patient satisfaction survey. Well, it was "free of charge".

Around 3:30 that afternoon, I was, finally, allowed to adjust my bed. Who would have ever thought that something so ostensibly insignificant as sitting upright would seem like such a godsend? That left only about a hundred other things that were still bothering me – multiple IVs in each arm, a gauze-wrapped hunk of lumber strapped to my right wrist (intended to immobilize it while the a-line remained inserted), disposable pulse-ox sensor taped to my middle finger on my left hand, heart monitor leads snaked strategically through my gown (ensuring that the slightest bit of motion would trigger uncomfortable tugging at the pads glued to my chest), blood pressure cuff sliding down over the elbow of my left arm, incessantly cycling pneumatic leg compression cuffs, and the Foley yanking at my bladder (and other things). The only upside to any of this was that I didn't have to struggle to use one of those hand-held urinals!

Wouldn't you know it, I spoke/thought too soon... the nurse came in and said that it was also time to remove the Foley catheter. I sure am glad that I was knocked out when the Foley was inserted, but if I had my druthers, I think I would have preferred to be knocked out for the removal. It's not that it was painful, exactly, but it was definitely not at all uncomfortable. My modesty, by the way... it was long gone by this time! At least, now, with the Foley out, I could get out of bed (still with a great deal of assistance rerouting the many tubes and wires that tethered me) if I wanted to go on a bold adventure and sit on the chair next to the bed instead of just sitting on the bed. In fact, I did this a couple of times throughout the rest of the day just because I could! And maybe for a slight change of scenery, too, as I could see out into the hall a little better from the chair (and hear what was going on around my corner of the ICU a little better, too).

Before my dinner had arrived, my EP stopped in to see me for the first time since the surgery to give me an update. He told me that everything went well and that it actually went quicker than he had expected – he had started just before 9:00 a.m. and finished after 3:00 p.m. So roughly six hours in total. He told me that I was transferred to the recovery room where I had to lie on my back with heavy sandbags on my groins for two hours (this is a standard procedure following any catheterization that is performed while the patient is on anticoagulants). He also said that he had talked to me in recovery as I was coming out of the anesthesia, and that I seemed conscious. Ah, but not so... I have absolutely no recollection of anything before waking up in the ICU. He seemed shocked to hear that. So that begs the question, what was I doing/saying before the time I *thought* I first woke up?

With my EP leaving as quickly as he had arrived, I decided to (you guessed it) watch some TV until my evening allotment of institutional foodstuff was delivered. All the while, the parade of techs and nurses through my room marched on – blood draws, x-rays, EKGs, echoes, oral meds, groin exams, and plantar blood flow checks. Oh, and now that the Foley catheter was out, there was one more wonderful annoyance added to that regemin – a regular ultrasound of my bladder. This was required, my nurse told me, for 24 hours following the removal of the Foley to ensure that my bladder was devoid of air and that it "remembered" how to contract properly after not needing to do so for so long. OK, if there was any last shred of modesty left, poof... now it was gone!

My heart had been good all this time, but early that evening, a familiar bout of atrial flutter kicked in. I literally paid no attention to it, not only because my EP told me to expect lots of arrhythmia for at least the next few months, but also because I was so used to being in constant flutter for nearly a month before my cardioversion that I, truly, hardly noticed it at all. My nurse didn't like it, though. I guess that's his job. He called my EP who promptly prescribed an increased dosage of amiodarone. My heart rate was rock-steady in the mid-130s, but overall, I was feeling pretty good. I had eaten most of my dinner that night and even entertained a few visiting friends before enjoying some pre-shuteye TV and, eventually, falling asleep... in flutter the whole time.

What I am going to tell you next, I am absolutely certain that you will not believe. What happened that night after I fell asleep, it might have been the most bizarre scene that I have ever witnessed in my entire life. It will sound completely fabricated, and if someone told it to me, I would not believe them. But I assure you, this really happened. It was around 2:30 a.m. I was disturbed from my slumber by a cacophony of loud voices, laughter, banging, and general noise. My room in the ICU was located right next to one of the entrances, and (much like my freshman dorm room in college) I could hear every time the door opened and closed. My room's clear glass interior wall allowed me to see just about everything that was going on in the immediate area, and what I saw going on was so shocking, I really almost thought that I was dreaming. Again, believe me, I swear that I was not.

There was a crowd of roughly fifteen rowdy young people, 20-somethings (who I at first assumed were probably nursing students from the dorms located right there on the hospital campus), that had literally stumbled in through the ICU doors and congregated at the front desk, which was just outside of my room. It was almost like an invasion. They were yelling and playing loud music and singing through the overhead paging system. I could hear them calling on the private intercoms into random rooms in the vicinity of mine, too. They held office chair races up and down the hall right outside my door, which quickly degenerated into more of an office chair demolition derby. Some of them were even picking up things off the counter and throwing them at each other. This entire crew definitely looked, sounded, and acted drunk. And given that the public bars and clubs around here are required to stop serving at 2:00 a.m., my assumption would seem to fit with the time that they arrived, too.

Besides just being generally disturbed by their behavior and baffled as to what they were doing there, how they got in, and why no one kicked them out, the worst part for me was when a couple of the guys came over to my room and looked on the computer at the nurses station right outside. I could hear one of them say in an affected voice, "Let's see what's wrong with Mr. Kauffman tonight." And they both laughed hysterically. I am not usually afraid of much of anything, but I was in a weakened state, tied to my bed by wires and tubes, and I feared that I would be almost completely helpless and not be able to defend myself should things get out of hand and they actually came into my room and wanted to play "doctor"! If they really were drunk, there's potentially no limit to what they might have tried to do. Right?

But just how did they even get into the ICU... there is very tight security to just get into the elevator that leads up to that floor. My visitors told me that they had to go to the security office in an entirely separate building on the hospital's campus and present their drivers licenses to get ID badges that would grant them access. The most bizarre part of the whole scene, however, was that the nurses on duty in the ICU that night completely ignored these marauders and turned a blind eye to their mayhem. When my overnight nurse did finally come in to do his regular checks of my IVs, etc., I bluntly asked him why no one was doing anything about them. He just looked away sheepishly and said "Yeah, sorry about that." It was as though he was embarrassed that the situation was beyond his control.

The nurse pulled the curtain across the glass front wall as he left the room, as if that was going to help. It actually made it worse for me, as now I couldn't see where the drunkards were or what they were doing, and I wouldn't be able to prepare for an onslaught, were one to occur. The other techs were still coming in regularly to do their tests during this time, and they all reacted in about the same way as my nurse did when I commented about the commotion. So apparently this was nothing new to them, either, and they seemed to feel helpless to do or even say anything about it. I started thinking that maybe these were not students but rather from a more privileged and protected strata... doctors' kids! That might better explain why they acted like, and indeed, seemed to be untouchable. Whoever they were, when their three-hour reign of terror ended, they left en masse as quickly as they came. I was pretty wound up by the whole experience and really wasn't able to sleep much afterwards.

Thursday, January 28th: I certainly didn't need to be awakened for my morning meds... I was already awake! Oh, and I was still in flutter, by the way. My EP stopped by before his office hours to check on me, and when he saw that the flutter was still going strong, he said, "I can't let you go home like this with a clear conscience." (All I got from that was that I was going home!) My EP didn't fool around... he wanted to zap me back into NSR right then and there before getting on with his day. No scheduling necessary! So the nurse wheeled in the ICU's old hand-me-down-looking defibrillator for him and handed him a hypodermic needle and a vial of fentanyl. No, not that dreaded "F" word! I reminded my EP of the TEE experience that I had on fentanyl just a few days earlier and asked if it were possible to get propafol. I was just asking... never hurts to ask, right? He very cheerfully said, "Sure." Out in the hall, I could hear him on the phone with anesthesiology trying to get a doctor and nurse to come up to my room to administer it. Meanwhile, his PA brought me a stack of consent forms to sign. The anesthesia team arrived, I got my propafol, and the procedure went off without a hitch. When I awoke moments later, everyone was gone, and my heart was in NSR. Whee!

A welcome breakfast soon followed, which I chose to enjoy from the considerably better vantage point of my chair. When I was finished, my nurse said that it was time to take a walk. He wanted to see that I was able to walk well enough before calling in someone from PT ("physical therapy") to evaluate me and give me the thumbs-up for discharge. Just getting ready to walk was quite an ordeal – unplug the IV meters, disconnect the a-line and pulse-ox sensor, remove the blood pressure cuff and calf cuffs, and up hook my heart monitor leads to a portable monitor that the nurse would tote behind me. I strapped on a secondary gown backwards for privacy (my nurse's idea), and then I took a stroll around the ICU. The ICU occupied the entire fourth floor of this wing of the hospital with rooms arranged along the outside walls (every room has a view!) and the nurses' areas and storage rooms all located in the center. The space between is a "hallway", of sorts, that goes 'round and 'round. That is where I perambulated.

My first steps out of the room were a bit unsteady, as I am sure you can imagine, and boy, did I feel weak. But after the first lap, I was gaining stamina and wanted to go again. The staff watched, cheering me on this time, and I felt quite ridiculous. But it was better than going back to my room where I had been imprisoned for what seemed like weeks. And then, to compound the embarrassment, I opted for a third lap. My nurse, even though he was a big guy, was, obviously, getting tired of hauling all the mobile equipment around behind me. Besides, as each nurse in the ICU is assigned to <u>two</u> patients, I am pretty sure that he probably had some other business that he needed to tend to. So begrudgingly, I let him lead me back to my room on our next pass. (OK, I did this... can I go home now???)

Just that few minutes of walking had me more than mildly exhausted, so I flopped down in the chair as the nurse reconnected all of my moorings - all but the blood pressure cuff. He left me to watch some TV for a while (zzzz) and then came back with [drum roll]... discharge papers. Yes, party time! I was a bit surprised, though, because it was only late-morning and not close to the magical 24 hours that I was originally told that I would have to wait after my Foley was pulled. I asked my nurse about it, and he just snorted, shrugged it off, and said that my bladder was fine - I take it that he didn't buy into the whole premise, either. There was still a small amount of seepage from my puncture sites, but that was most likely due to my getting up and walking. My heart was thankfully still in NSR, and all of my latest tests looked good. The word came down from above (I assume) that there was no need for me to be there anymore, and I am pretty sure that the ICU staff was as happy to be getting rid of me as I was to be leaving.

But before going over the discharge papers with me, my nurse had to remove my arterial line. He pulled out the other multiple IVs first and then removed the pulse-ox sensor and heart monitor pads. Then he asked me to sit on the bed, and he spread a huge tarp across my lap, most of the bed, and what seemed like about half of the room. He lined up various supplies across this tarp so they'd be handy when he needed them, donned gloves and a face shield, and told me to look away. Of course I'm not going to look away... I'm paying for this! I didn't want to miss anything. And there would be a lot to miss.

First, he unwrapped the yards of tape immobilizing my wrist against the wooden board and pulled off enough bandages to treat a shotgun wound. With the area of interest now exposed, he held a big wad of gauze perched over the a-line entry point on my wrist, and in one swift and less-than-graceful motion, he pulled the tube out with one hand and lost control of the gauze that he was holding in the other... in perfect sync with my heart beat, no less. A jet of blood shot out from my wrist reminiscent of Spiderman. Seriously, it seemed as though it had the force of a high-capacity water pistol. The blood hit the nurse's hand that was still holding the tube, and it sprayed every which way. Now I understand why they wear the face shield. His quick reaction limited the mess to a single spritz, as he quickly retrieved the gauze and got it into position before the next eruption. Then, with about ten minutes to kill while he kept considerable pressure on my wrist to stop the bleeding (remember, I was on warfarin), we engaged in idle chat. While I am always up for that, at that point I really just wanted to get out of there.

My blood had the decency to clot just in time for the guy from PT to arrive. He watched me stand up and walk a few steps, and then his work was done there! I waded through the stack of nondescript paperwork that my nurse had collated for me and signed off on everything. I thought that would be it... time to go. Fortunately, I hadn't yet called on my brother to come for me because the nurse (somehow) noticed that there was a missing page in my discharge packet. He said that it could be a while and that he might as well order some lunch for me. More hospital food... what a special treat! And with that, came more boring mid-weekday TV. The missing page arrived in due time, and then I called my brother. About 15 minutes later, I was transported by wheelchair down to the loading dock... interesting that I didn't have to walk at all, so why did PT have to evaluate my walking before I could leave? Policy is policy, I suppose. When the door to the parking garage opened, I was surprised by the cold weather. Yes, I knew that it was mid-January, but when I had arrived only three days before, it had been a freakishly warm day for what is normally the coldest time of the year around here, and now it was about 30 degrees cooler. But who cares... I was out of there!

I was never so happy to be back in my own home as I was that day. I still didn't feel great, but my mental state was much better there. I had already planned on doing nothing at all for a few days except keep an eye on the puncture sites in my groins, as instructed, and call the cardiology office if there was any pain or signs of bleeding or swelling. So I stayed in bed as much as possible – TV on and laptop and phone at my side – to keep my legs elevated and to minimize the amount of hip joint movement so that the blood vessels could heal (the idea of my femoral veins opening up and me bleeding out into my legs might have been the scariest part of the whole procedure for me!).

When there was still seepage from one of the puncture sites the next day, I called my EP. He asked me about the flow. Flow? What did he mean by that? He wanted to know if it was a trickle or just a drip. It was at that moment that I realized that I had probably overreacted, and maybe I shouldn't have called. I told him, "Neither." No flow, just some seepage. He kind of chuckled and assured me that it was normal and nothing at all to worry about. But he told me that, if I did have more *significant* bleeding, I should get some heavy bags of rice and lie flat on my back for a few hours with them on my groins. Since I didn't have any heavy bags of rice in the house, and I wasn't supposed to drive for at least ten days, I was hoping that I would not have to resort to this home clotting remedy. But at least now I knew what to do should the need arise.

A long, uneventful week of sitting in my bed had gone by when my EP called to check up on me. I told him that the seepage had stopped, but I did have a significant amount of pain in both groins. There was no swelling that I could see, but he said that, because I was heavy, I might not see the swelling if there were any. He didn't sound too concerned, but he did ask me to come in so he could have a look. This would be my first time driving since before I went in for the procedure, and it was a few days ahead of what my discharge instructions allowed (they said to avoid lifting, stairs, and driving for 10 to 14 days).

When I arrived at the cardiology office, I didn't need to check in because it wasn't a real appointment (and there was no charge!). I was immediately taken back to a small side room to wait for my EP. He came in between his regular appointments to give me a quick once-over. He pressed painfully hard in both groins to check for any major pockets of blood. He found none, everything seemed normal. When he asked me how much exercise I had been getting. I told him, uh... basically none. Well, seems like that was the whole problem. Getting up and walking around, exercising the thigh muscles, helps to work the leaked blood out of the interstitial spaces in the muscle tissue. The pressure this blood puts on surrounding tissue causes the pain, just like inflammation would. Moving around a little more should disperse the blood and relieve the pain. Made sense to me.

After that, I tried to stand and walk as much as possible. And it really seemed to help in just a few days. But I still hadn't taken a shower. I continued to bathe out of the sink because I didn't want to get my groins or wrist wet until they were fully healed (remember, I was paranoid about these wounds opening and bleeding uncontrollably because I was still on warfarin). I also continued to sleep in the middle of my bed with pillows propping me up on both sides to keep me from rolling in my sleep. I thought that too much motion while sleeping might pop something open, too. The story of one of my parents' neighbors bleeding to death in her sleep when her dialysis shunt came out kept popping into my mind. I knew this was completely unrelated to my condition and a totally irrational fear, but I still thought that "better safe than sorry" was a prudent axiom to follow.

Another uneventful week passed, and the groin pains were much less noticeable. I also started to see bruising on my thighs. This is normal and is caused by the blood that leaks out into the muscle tissue during and after the procedure finally dispersing. And hallelujah, I began taking showers this week... probably the single greatest step that I took towards feeling somewhat human again. I also began driving more regularly and basically just tried to get back to a pretty normal life in all respects. It was a good thing, too, because I was already past-due to have my INR tested at my cardiology group's "Coumadin® Clinic". They were starting to panic and called to remind me every day. I was pretty sure I was OK, though, as long as I wasn't bleeding. After all, that's the *only* thing that I cared about!

When on warfarin (Coumadin®), regular blood tests are required to make sure the proper level of anticoagulation is maintained. The range of INR values that provides the desired amount of protection while also minimizing the risk of clotting too slowly is known as the "therapeutic range" (a higher INR means less chance of a clot forming, but it also increases the risk of potentially dangerous bleeding). The therapeutic range that my EP wanted my INR to be in was 2.0 to 3.0. Because of the way warfarin works, the patient must adhere to certain dietary rules to keep his/her INR in range. There are a few restricted items that should be avoided altogether, but even things that are not restricted can cause significant variations in your INR. Other medications, for example, can cause fluctuations, as can stress and exercise. The most important thing, in general, is consistency... consistency of diet and of lifestyle. If you eat and do the same things every day, in theory, your INR should remain stable and your dosage should not have to be adjusted. It can be very touchy, and it is really hard to know, for sure, what will have an effect and what kind of effect it might have until you do it. But with experience, your INR should become easier to regulate.

For me, I found that, when my INR would go very low, below therapeutic range (closer to untreated blood), which left me at a higher risk for a clot, my dosage would be increased to compensate for whatever caused my INR to drop. Then, at my next visit, my INR would be too high (putting me at risk for bleeding), so the dosage would be decreased. One of the biggest lifestyle problems this posed was that, whenever a change was made to my dosage, I would have to go back and get retested in just 4 or 5 days. If it would have remained more stable, I would have been able to go in only once a week or every 10 days. And if a patient's INR remains very stable for a long period of time, some only have to get tested once every two to four weeks. I wasn't on it long enough for that to happen, but I would have been happy with testing just once a week. (The NOAs, or "novel oral anticoagulants", were not yet available at this time. More on them later.)

In addition to these INR testing woes, there was one other problem that had popped up. I only began noticing it about a week after I got home from the hospital. A vein on the top of my right hand was swollen and very painful. It was the vein through which my IV amiodarone was administered. As days passed, the portion of the vein that was swollen was getting longer, progressing upward toward my wrist. It was getting more painful, as well, especially as it passed my wrist and continued to swell up my arm. This happened around the end of February, about one month after my procedure. I didn't think it was an infection, because an infection would have shown up just a few days after the IV was pulled. But I didn't care what it was, exactly. It hurt and kept me from using my wrist, so I had to have it taken care of.

Who ya gonna call? I called my EP about it, of course. He didn't want to diagnose it over the phone, so he told me to go see the hospital's IV team – he gave me the phone number for their hot-line. The nurse that I spoke with there told me to come in to the ER and just give them my name at the desk... they'd be waiting for me. I was dreading spending another long night in the ER, but when I arrived and told them who I was, I was taken right back to a room with no paperwork or insurance forms to fill out! A nurse came in right away and looked at my hand. She also suspected that it was not infected (it was not red or hot), but she wasn't sure what was causing the swelling. So she grabbed an ER doc to come take a look at it. And the doctor didn't seem to know what it was, either, but I did take the opportunity to get some free professional advice about a few other things that had been bothering me. One was a lump on the extensor tendon of my middle finger of my right hand that is sometimes there and sometimes not. It was not painful but plainly visible on top of my hand (and very near the offending vein). She identified this lump as a ganglion cyst (ah, one more thing for me to research). I also asked her about my hands turning bright red or pale white from the cold. She told me that it could be Raynaud's Syndrome but was more likely caused by the metoprolol that I was taking... beta blockers are known to cause similar symptoms. After our little chat, I was free to go... no paperwork. And I was never billed. Best ER visit ever!

The next two months passed without incident. I noticed that my post-procedural arrhythmias were dwindling, as I was told to expect. I received paperwork in April for my first quarterly blood test to monitor the damage caused by the amiodarone that I was still on (this was actually eleven different blood tests), and I received an order for a pulmonary function test (this test only has to be performed once after starting amiodarone). I went for both of these tests and then, at my first official post-procedural follow up at the end of the month, I found out that my pulmonary function looked good (meaning no lung damage from the amiodarone) and the blood tests came back OK, too. My liver enzymes were on the rise, though, and in light of this, and considering that my a-fib had all-but disappeared by this point, we decided to stop the amiodarone and see how things went for the next three months. If I stayed in NSR, then it would be time to consider stopping the warfarin, too. I was happy to finally be on the path towards reducing the number of meds that I was on. That's why I had the surgery, after all!

And this was especially true for warfarin. I was still having difficulty regulating my INR. At one point, it went up to almost five. The nurse in the clinic told me that an INR of five isn't necessarily bad – she has seen some go up near 20 or more with no problems. And some patients are kept at five or higher depending upon the condition that they take the warfarin for. That did make me feel a little better, until a few days later when I noticed some black in my stools. They were not altogether "black and tarry", the classic indication of large amounts of digested blood. But since I was very careful to keep my diet consistent, this change could have been a sign of trace amounts of blood coming from the upper GI tract. I reported it to my EP, and even though it did not persist, he thought it would be best to have it checked out. He was a "better safe than sorry" guy, too. And it was only May – he wanted me to be able to stay on the warfarin for at least another two months. So he definitely wanted any suspected bleeding to be checked out.

The following week, I saw a gastroenterologist. I told her my whole story and why I was there, to which she simply replied

"We [gastroenterologists] hate warfarin". She wanted to do an EGD to check for bleeding, but said that they would only do it if I could stop the warfarin for five days. I got my EP's OK on this, and we did the EGD. It was very much like the EGD that I had done almost seven years earlier. And there were no indications of any bleeding found. Part of the history that I gave the gastroenterologist included the upper-right abdominal pain that I was still having for the last ten years. She ordered a hepatobiliary (HIDA) scan with CCK (cholecystokinin, a hormone that regulates digestion of fat and protein by, among other things, controlling the release of bile from the gall bladder). This was a nuclear medicine test that involved the injection of a radioactive isotope, similar to the cardiac perfusion scans that I had had almost two years earlier.

The doctor also sent me for an upper-GI CT scan, which involved drinking two very large cups of water (laced with an iodine-based contrast agent) over a 45 minute period, followed by one more cup chugged down just before lying on the table. The scan itself, just like the one of my heart, took only a few seconds. Another abdominal ultrasound then rounded out my package of GI tests. And at the follow up with the doctor... [drum roll, please] no problems found. The doctor said that the pain might or might not be related to bleeding, if I actually had any bleeding, and that it could also be any of a thousand other things. She said that the only way to know for sure would be to wait for it to get worse. How comforting. Ah, yes... thousands of dollars, well spent.

It was now early June. Besides the GI hullabaloo, I was feeling pretty good being off of the amiodarone. My a-fib was practically gone (*Figure 3, page 253*), and it was time to do some catching up on life. I made plans to get together with a friend who I hadn't seen in quite some time. Her teenage daughter and her daughter's friend wanted to tag along, so we decided to spend the afternoon at a local "family fun" restaurant that has a big game-room in the back. We chowed down and then made a beeline for the games. I still had not recovered fully from the effects of years of a-fib (especially the associated weight gain) or from my recent surgery, but the girls didn't care. They had me running around, often in two directions at once, it seemed, until I was exhausted and had no choice but to be the party-pooper. Back at the house, I must have looked like easy prey to them – an impromptu, high-spirited, two-on-one wrestling match broke out (really just me trying to defend myself against their onslaught). The girls won by default when I felt a sudden, sharp pain in the vicinity of my suspected abdominal hernia. I capitulated but never mentioned anything about the pain to them. I felt it would be prudent to have a doctor take a look at it, though.

So I called a general surgeon the next day, and he saw me posthaste. He checked me out and said that I did, indeed, have a small hernia. It was not yet an emergency, and the pain that I was feeling was just from the torn muscle tissue and not because there was any bowel protruding through, but he recommended repairing it soon before it got any worse. Of course, he would not do the surgery while I was on warfarin. He wanted me off the warfarin for at least three days prior to the surgery and then for ten days after. I called my EP to get his OK before stopping the warfarin, but I got even better news. My EP said that I should just stop the warfarin altogether since I had only had a few bouts of a-fib over the past two months and since each bout had only lasted a few minutes. No more trips to the clinic, and one month ahead of schedule. Great news!

Relative to everything else that I had just been through, the hernia surgery truly was a "piece of cake" (yes, I am aware that I use that expression too much). Actually, relative to nothing at all, it was quite easy, too. It was an out-patient procedure performed laparoscopically with only three tiny incisions (one of which was in the navel so that you can't even see the scar). The surgery was performed at a relatively new doctor-owned facility that boasted no patient infections in their three years of operation (as compared to the very high rate of infection reported at the local hospital). In fact, they were so confident of the sterility of their facility that they didn't even put me on antibiotics following the surgery.

I did feel a bit nauseated after coming out of the anesthesia, so I was given a shot of Compazine® (prochlorperazine) to relieve the symptom. I'm not sure if it was supposed to, but it knocked me out cold. But at least I didn't feel the nausea! They must have really needed my bed in the recovery room, though, because as soon as I fell asleep – it seemed like it, anyway (actually more than an hour later!) – they ever-so-rudely roused me, rushed me to get dressed, and pointed me toward the door. I was really unsteady on my feet and felt like I was about to fall over more than a couple of times. But I could deal with that. More importantly, I had absolutely no pain at all afterwards, just some significant bruising of the "nether regions" as the interstitial blood worked its way out. One week later, I had a follow up with the doctor, and that was it... back to normal. Quite a contrast to my ablation.

Around the same time as the hernia surgery, I started to experience periodic severe dizzy spells. It sometimes seemed to be related to some sort of visual disturbance, but not always. Maybe it was *causing* these visual disturbances. I had been accustomed to having sinus problems my whole life, but none like this. Still, I thought that my sinuses and/or inner ear might be the culprit. I decided to experiment with some home remedies on my own before seeing yet another doctor (I am sure that my insurance company was about to send a lynch mob after me for racking up almost $100,000 in charges already in just the first half of the year). So I tried using a steam vaporizer with essential oils, menthol throat lozenges, strong mints and chewing gum, and a Neti pot to flush out my nasal passages. I had varying degrees of success with each of these, and the results were very inconsistent. Sometimes my regimen seemed to help, but other times, not so much. So I wasn't entirely convinced that either my sinuses or my inner ear were to blame for the dizziness. I guess I would have to eventually see another doctor about it.

But I made the best of it for the time being, just thankful that my a-fib was a thing of the past. My activity level had increased quite a bit, and I was slowly losing some of excess the weight that I had gained without even trying. The next few weeks would be uneventful, for the most part, which enabled me to enjoy the nice summer weather, get some work done around the house, and spend time hanging out and having fun with my family and friends – all things that I had not been able to do for more than three years while atrial fibrillation had my life on hold.

FRUSTRATION

I am glad that I enjoyed those few uneventful weeks, but at the same time, I am also a bit peeved that I allowed myself to enjoy them. In hindsight, I may have been too quick to take the "feeling well" for granted, because when I was suddenly slammed with a twelve-hour-long bout of atrial flutter, I was really thrown for a loop. (I would, later, learn that this was *left* atrial flutter, a not-too-uncommon side effect of the PVI). During this bout, my heart rate was a bit higher than I had become accustomed to prior to the PVI – the mid-160s. Even though it did eventually stop on its own and didn't seem like it would return any time soon, I still felt myself turning back into that person that I was before... wanting to stay home "just in case". But I tried to fight it and think that maybe it was just a fluke. Ah, wishful thinking at its best.

All was quiet for the next few weeks, and I began feeling comfortable enough to return to my musician-adjacent days of yore when the opportunity arose to take on the job of sound man for an outdoor gig that my friend's band was putting on. It really did seem like that single, long bout of flutter *was* just a fluke. Wrong! I ended up having bouts on about half of the days in the last two weeks of August. Most were under an hour long, but a few lasted for several hours. It was a cruel flash back to the non-life that I thought I had left behind, and I began to become withdrawn again. I guess this was in anticipation of, or in preparation for, the condition to worsen to the level that it was before. But the next month, September, was about the same with relatively short bouts of flutter on about half of the days. The bouts *were* slowly growing longer, and a few bouts of a-fib crept back in, as well. I was still in denial, however, and I committed to producing, recording, mixing, and publishing this same band's first studio album. I thought that it should at least keep my mind off of the sense of "impending doom". NOTE: Never under-estimate the power of distraction!

But I was granted a brief reprieve from the arrhythmias for a while, suffering only one bout in the first three weeks of October. This allowed me to concentrate on my job and on the rest of my life as it led up to my next follow-up visit with my EP. At that appointment, I told him about the flutter and a-fib that I had been experiencing. It was his feeling that, since I was still within that magical one-year post-surgical healing period, these things were to be expected and, therefore, were unremarkable. And since the bouts were spaced irregularly and still fairly short, he was more optimistic than I and was not ready to say that this was a sign that the chronic condition was returning. He told me just to stay vigilant and to call him if it were to suddenly become worse or if I developed any different symptoms. Fair enough. (Remember to follow along on *Figure 3, page 253*.)

Just a few days later, and in light of my EP's apparent lack of concern, I decided to put my own concerns on the back burner and joined my friends on a four-day camping trip. I'm talking real tent camping. In the woods. I had never done it before, so I figured it would at least be a new experience for me. There wasn't much of anything else to do other than to collect and chop wood, tend the fire, eat, and drink. But I still had fun... I find just sitting around in the woods doing nothing at all (but talking!) to be very relaxing. We brought lots of eggs, bacon, burgers, and hot dogs to cover our meals along with large quantities of beer and booze. After a few days of constant, unrestrained gluttony and semi-heavy drinking punctuated by 30°F late-October nights spent trying to sleep on the hard, rocky ground, the flutter and a-fib set in again. Of course, given the way we were living on this trip, my first thought was that I was simply suffering from just another case of holiday heart.

But acute bouts of a-fib that are referred to as holiday heart usually stop when whatever triggered them is removed. Mine continued for the duration of our vacation, on through the last week of October, and into the first couple of weeks of November. This time, the bouts were many hours long – sometimes lasting all day – and much more severe in terms of heart rate, palpitations, and general discomfort (both physical and psychological). By the end of November, though, and as quickly as they came on, the bouts calmed back down considerably. OK, they were still worse than what they had been in September and October, but it's all relative. And, with the holiday season around the corner, I was thankful for whatever relief came my way!

January and February 2011: Not-so-happy New Year. These were bad months for me. My stress level was high, as a dear friend of almost 20 years, hospitalized numerous times over the previous four months for addiction-related health issues, finally succumbed to the years of self-abuse. Did this have an effect my arrhythmia? Perhaps... the four weeks from mid-January to mid-February were particularly bad for me as I was in nearly constant a-fib and flutter during that time. It was worse than any that I had ever had before. I did my best to just tough it out – after all, I had the experience to do so. But around 11:00 p.m. on February 19th, I just could not take it anymore. My heart rate had been in the low-200s for some time, and I felt that it was time to take a road trip to the ER. I actually felt fine, completely asymptomatic, but I found the high rate to be a bit scary... I didn't know how high was too high, and I didn't want to find out! So I followed my rule of thumb – better safe than sorry. (I guess if I really wanted to play it safe, I wouldn't have driven myself to the ER... not this time or any of the other times!)

I must say that this was one bizarre ER visit. There's a whole other story to be told about this one particular night (my next book?), but I will try to summarize it for you here. I was put in a room at a busy hallway intersection where there seemed to be a lot of passersby, and nearly every one of them spotted my heart rate on the gigantic flat-screen monitor above my head and, if there was no one else in the room with me at the time, they'd stop to ask me if I was alright. Yes! (Just leave me alone!) I felt fine. As I said, completely asymptomatic. I only came to the ER because I was a chicken... OK? While I was there, as many as two people at once were working on starting IVs on both of my arms, but neither could find my veins. Someone came in to get an EKG, too. When a doctor finally came in, I gave him my whole medical history. He, quickly and confidently, said that this (my fast heart rate) was definitely <u>not</u> related to my atrial fibrillation or any of my other recent medical history. He told me that this was, most likely, a case of ventricular tachycardia (or "v-tach"). Anything ventricular is usually bad (except those pesky PVCs, of course), so I *really* did not want it to be that. It couldn't be that. Could it?

But fear is <u>not</u> why I told him that I was 100% sure that it was atrial flutter. I knew it was flutter by the classic humming or buzzing sensation in my chest. I thought if he would just listen to my heart, then he would know it, too. It was immediately obvious, though, that his mind was already made up and that he did not appreciate my suggestion. He just looked at me as if I were an idiot and said that if it were atrial flutter, then that would mean that my atrial rate would be at least double the ventricular rate, or about 420 beats per minute in this case, and that it was physically impossible for the atria to beat that fast. He was so sure of himself and acted quite proud of his most astute observation.

He actually *was* correct... the atria <u>cannot</u> beat that fast. What he was ignorant of, apparently, is that the atria **do not beat** when in atrial flutter – they only vibrate in place. But the physical limitations that prevent the atria from beating that rapidly does not stop the electrical signals from cycling through the tissue at that high of a rate. I firmly stood my ground and plead my case with him, especially because I knew that he was leaning towards defibrillation, and I did not want to be needlessly zapped – the fewer high-voltage shocks to the heart in one lifetime, the better off you are! So the indignant doctor turned and walked out without a word, just a maddening, cocky grin on his face. He came back in a minute or two later with a syringe of something in his hand and a big smile on his face. I guess he would show me a thing or two! He proclaimed that what he held in his hand was adenosine (I could have guessed that) and that it would slow down my heart's ventricular rate enough so the p-wave (atrial contractions) would be easier to see on the monitor. If the p-wave was normal, it would confirm that I had a ventricular arrhythmia. It was then that I told him flat out that smart money was on an abnormally fast p-wave. Wow, he sure didn't seem to like me, and the feeling was mutual.

Dr. Smartypants asked me if I had ever had adenosine before, and I said, "Oh yeah. I'm ready." You must mentally prepare for it, like a roller coaster ride. Adenosine slows your heart rate down and makes your blood vessels relax and dilate. This can cause intense flushing all over the body. And as the oxygen level of your blood goes up, you might begin feeling dizzy, lights may seem brighter, and you may hear buzzing or ringing sounds. Adenosine can also cause temporary bronchospasms, which can make breathing seem difficult. But these effects only last while the adenosine is being administered – once the injection stops, things instantly (more or less) return to normal. And when you are lying down and already in the hospital, it can be a very interesting experience. Knowing that you are safe no matter what happens, you can *almost* enjoy it. Almost!

Here it comes, the moment of truth. I wish that I actually had put money on this. In went the adenosine. I closed my eyes (because I knew that the already bright lights would likely blind me, and I knew that I wouldn't need to see the monitor to know the result), and then the good doctor said "Hmm... I think I need to use more. I didn't get a good look at the p-wave." I think he was really just trying to torture me for disagreeing with him. Bring it on! And with an evil grin, he administered the second and even larger dose, I rode the roller coaster, and when I opened my eyes, his face had completely changed. The cockiness was gone. He looked like the decent human that he probably once was. And his words at that moment still ring pleasingly in my memory to this day: "Looks like you were right... it *is* flutter." Well, I guess I am not as dumb as I look. No, I didn't say that, but I should have. I wouldn't have had time to, though, because he hauled his butt out of there in shame, toot sweet, and never returned. Please understand that I normally have the utmost respect for doctors of all kinds and for the work that they do, but this guy really rubbed me the wrong way. And he ever so clearly illustrated the reason for my cardiologists' disdain for the ER staff and their practices.

So OK... flutter confirmed. A nurse came in and put me on IV amiodarone. Hmm, maybe I would have rather been zapped! Drip, drip, drip went the amio... for quite a while, but to no avail. I am now going to skip the ensuing theatrics that occurred right outside my room for my viewing pleasure during this time. First, an unkempt mother and her young-adult son taken into a conference room across the hall from me by a police officer arguing very loudly whenever the officer left the room – the mother threatening to tell the cop what the son was "on" and the son calling his mother every name in the book. And then, there was the belligerent guest that was literally dragged into the room next to mine. After things began crashing against the walls and flying out into the hall, screams for assistance were answered by police, EMTs, orderlies, anyone up for some action, and I assume, a sedative-wielding nurse, because the subject was subdued shortly thereafter. Better than anything on TV, for sure!

Later, two very Doogie Howser-esque residents came in to chat with me. I don't know if they were just really bored in the ER at 1:00 a.m. or if they were "assigned" to monitor me, but they asked lots of questions and seemed to be really interested in my education, my employment history, the story of my a-fib of course, and in all the many other stories that I told them (I'm always sure to make good use of an audience whenever I have one). My flutter chugged along this whole time, undaunted by the meds, and the residents eventually left and came back with a shot of digoxin for me. I promptly fought against it (remember, my EP said that digoxin was a big no-no with a-fib... and my own experience proved that). But Doogie #1 explained to me that it was not being administered as a maintenance drug – they just wanted to try a single dose to temporarily bring my heart rate down while I waited for the amio to kick in. So I caved, but I told him that nothing had ever worked to significantly bring my rate down while in flutter before. I guess we'll see. So in went the digoxin. Bonk! You guessed it... it did not slow my rate down one bit. They were stumped. (I seem to have that effect on a lot of people.)

By 3:00 a.m., I had been in left atrial flutter for roughly six hours. This was long enough to catch the doctor's attention. He ordered heparin in an Oz-like fashion (from "behind the curtain"). If you recall, I had already been off of warfarin for quite some time. But getting heparin meant that I would have to be admitted, and so I was whisked away to another room somewhere in a distal building. There was a patient sleeping in the next bed when I arrived, but I was wide awake – hello TV, my old friend. But then a nurse came in to go through the admissions paperwork with me. Ugh! And then the heparin bag was hung by the amio, with care, in hopes that sinus rhythm soon would be there. And in about an hour, I had converted! Once a nurse finally woke up and took note of this, my amiodarone and heparin were promptly stopped. But I'd still have to wait for a cardiologist to see me before being discharged. It was almost 5:00 a.m., and it had been a looong and exhausting night. Maybe I could get a little sleep before the doctor stopped by. Please?

Nope. Once again, the adage is proven – there truly is no rest for the weary. The guy in the next bed decided to wake up just then and start talking to me. I felt delirious and don't even remember what I said to him. The curtains had been left open, and now the sun was coming up, and I just wanted to sleep. What better time for breakfast to arrive? This was almost getting to be funny. I had one thing on my mind... sleep! So I didn't even touch the food. Finally, the doctor made an appearance. He talked to the man in the next bed first, and then stopped by to tell me that I had a bout of atrial flutter and that I should see an EP. I stopped him as he began to explain flutter to me, gave him a synopsis of my history with it, and told him that I was already seeing an EP, and that it was one of his colleagues. And with that, he just said "OK" and told me that I could go home. Since I was already officially discharged that morning and had just been waiting for the doctor to show up, no lunch had been ordered for me. But my discharge paperwork was delayed and didn't arrive until almost 2:00 p.m. I don't know which was worse, hunger so bad that I wished for hospital food or the want of sleep. Alas, I got neither. The nurse presented me with the stack when it arrived, which I promptly leafed through and signed (and signed, and...), and then I was finally free to go home. What a long, strange trip it had been. Can I sleep now???

Two days later, my EP, having caught wind of my impromptu adventure, called me in to see him. I shared with him the story of this most recent ER experience and presented to him my current post-ablation arrhythmia chart (*Figure 3, page 253*). After first reiterating his contempt for ER doctors and the ER in general, he explained to me the difference between "left atrial flutter", which he suspected that I now suffered from, and the more common and much slower "right atrial flutter" that I had been experiencing prior to the ablation. Since he had already performed a specialized ablation in my right atrium (a single circumferential lesion, which is generally very successful) to eradicate the right flutter at the same time that he performed the PVI for my a-fib, he was fairly certain that what I now suffered from was left atrial flutter. This left flutter, according to him, was a not-too-uncommon side effect of the PVI and often more persistent than right flutter, resistant to treatment with drugs, and slower to stop on its own. So... frying pan to fire?

Since I had already had the ablation, he thought that just an antiarrhythmic medication might help to keep the flutter in check. Having had literally no success at all with *any* of the antiarrhythmics that we had tried except for amiodarone, amio would have been the natural first choice. However, I would only now learn that my liver enzymes had started to rise the last time that I was on amio, so he was hesitant to prescribe it for me again. But dronedarone (Multaq®) had just recently become available. Dronedarone was sort of an "amiodarone lite" that did not contain iodine, but rather a sulfonamide group in its stead. It was purported to be a safer, but nearly as effective alternative to amiodarone.

I knew someone who had been on Multaq® post-ablation, and it had worked well for him with no side-effects, so I figured that I'd give it a try. But there's always a hitch. Being new to the market, there was no generic dronedarone available yet, and my insurance would not cover its cost (which was very high... several dollars per dose). In light of this fact, my EP stealthily led me down a labyrinth of secluded corridors leading to their samples vault (more like just a locked closet) where he surreptitiously filled two of the practice's complimentary logo-emblazoned zippered totes with every last Multaq® sample that they had on hand (71 of them, to be exact). I felt inclined to hide them in the lining of my jacket on my way out of the office!

After just a few days on the dronedarone, all went quiet on the cardiac front. But then after one full week on this new medication, I suddenly developed a blurred spot in the very center of my field of vision. It occurred while I was operating the mixing board during a recording session with the band. The blurred spot grew and, for lack of a better description, began to twinkle or sparkle. As it continued to grow outward, it changed from just a spot into the shape of a backwards letter "C". This might have freaked me out more than anything else in my life ever had, but I tried to keep working without letting on that anything was bothering me. (Remember... the power of distraction!) I had no other symptoms, so I figured that I would just try to wait it out.

After all, the show must go on! And after 15 to 20 minutes, the anomaly had drifted to the outer edges of my vision and then beyond, where it just disappeared.

That was on a Sunday, so I couldn't call my eye doctor's office until the next day... which I did (even though it had been more than ten years since my last visit). I was able to get an appointment with one of their MDs that same afternoon. She checked my eyes and said that everything looked normal and healthy. Based, solely, on my description of the symptoms that I had had, she concluded that what I had experienced was an ocular migraine. The optic nerve, in fact, is not a nerve at all, but it along with the retina and the entire eye itself are really just outgrowths of the brain, so anything that can happen in the brain can also happen in the eye. The funny thing is that, after I got this what seemed to me like a very strange and rare diagnosis, I mentioned it to some of my friends and family and learned that quite a few of them had either also experienced this at some point in their lives or continue to experience it on a regular basis. I guess, like anything else, you just get used to it. Or maybe it is just the kind of thing that is so weird that no one talks about. I talk to everyone about everything, and this case is a good example of why... I usually learn something from it!

After this strange and unexpected betrayal by my eye, I had a few more days of flutter and a-fib, but then nothing but smooth sailing NSR for more than a month. Could it be? Is the dronedarone really working that well? Why do I let myself think these silly things? Just as I was getting comfortable with the idea that Multaq® was the answer to my problems, the fibs and flutters started up again. They only lasted about an hour, though, and then nothing again for a few more days. I thought (hoped) that that would be the end of it, but like a bad penny, it came back to me. I figured that if this bout only lasted an hour and then stopped on its own like the last one did, then it wouldn't be too bad... I could easily live with just a little of this every few days if I had to. Little did I know when it started, though, how much of an impact this one particular bout of a seemingly-mundane arrhythmia was going to have on the rest of my life.

Frustration

From Bad to Worse

The day was April 21, 2011. I will always remember this date. It would turn out to be the start of what led to possibly the worst event of my life -- an event that, ironically, might have then led to the best decision that I have ever made. On this day, a bout of atrial flutter started around 7:30 p.m. It wasn't a particularly notable bout with a rate around the mid-150s. By this time, after more than four years of palpitations from a-fib and flutter, I had become an expert at ignoring most sensations in my chest, so I went about my normal evening activities and eventually to bed without giving them a second thought. Sleeping as well as I could, all things considered, I did wake up several times throughout the night. Each time, I noted that I was still in flutter. But none of this was at all out of the ordinary for me.

I awoke on the morning of April 22nd still in flutter. I did some work, and then I went to meet a friend for lunch. I was in flutter the entire time while driving to the restaurant and while eating my lunch. I left the restaurant around 1:30 that afternoon, and just as I got in my car and prepared to return home, the flutter stopped. It was like throwing a switch. Poof... NSR. That was a little strange, in hindsight, because my flutter usually degenerated into a-fib first, however briefly. So anyway, it totalled about an 18-hour bout – nowhere near the longest that I had ever had, but it was the longest bout that I had had in at least few months. I was really just glad that it was over, though. And I felt fine.

Happily back in NSR, I drove back home. I got right back to the work that I was doing before lunch, and then sometime around 3:00 p.m. I got an email from a friend who I hadn't talked to in some time. So I decided to take a quick break and give her a call. I had been doing my work on my laptop, sitting on my living room sofa with my feet up and shoes off. The TV was on but muted. Heart is in NSR for over an hour now. I put my laptop down on the seat next to me, picked up my cell phone, and made the call to my friend. As we began to catch up and enjoyed a pleasant conversation, I could not possibly have imagined – not even in my wildest dreams (or rather, *nightmares*) – what would happen next.

These symptoms that I am about to describe came on all at once. The first thing that I really noticed was that my friend's voice sounded garbled in my left ear, the ear that I was holding the phone to. It was my cell phone, so a garbled voice, alone, wasn't terribly unusual. But the ambient sounds (mostly of splashing water and bubbles coming from my aquarium in the far corner of the room) also seemed different. I became totally distracted, (rudely) stopped paying attention to my friend, and un-muted the TV. The voices on the TV were garbled, too... this couldn't be good! And I noticed that, when I looked at the TV, everything had a twinkly or sparkly appearance to it very much like the visual disturbance that I had experienced with the ocular migraine, but this time it was not confined to just one spot or a "C" shape – this time, it affected my entire field of vision. And I also felt a tingling sensation in the entire left side of my body, particularly my left arm and left leg. It was the exact sensation that you might get from sitting on your wallet, for example, restricting the blood flow to your leg. But this was in my arm *and* leg at the same time. And to get this in conjunction with the other symptoms....... **NOT. GOOD.**

Keep in mind that all of these came on simultaneously and in just a split second, but as is often the case during many traumatic events, it seems to me now as though it happened in slow motion. (This is actually a real thing, by the way... it is caused by adrenaline speeding up your brain's time reference so that things are processed at a greater temporal resolution and, hence, seems slower. This allows the brain to analyze more details in an emergency.) So the way that I just described it in the last paragraph is the way that it *seemed* to happen, but it really was probably no more than a second or two before I realized that these were stroke symptoms. I (even more rudely) hung up on my friend (which as I later learned, she just assumed was a bad cell phone connection) and got up from the sofa. That's when I noticed another symptom... poor sense of balance. Very dizzy and unsteady, I made my way to the kitchen, grabbed my landline home phone, and dialed 911 (this is the only reason that I still pay for home phone service, by the way). Don't ask me why, but the next thing that I did after requesting an ambulance was feed my fish. I guess it was more of a reaction than a conscious decision... I must have subconsciously known that I'd be away from home for a while. Then I came back to the sofa to put on my shoes, and by that time the ambulance had arrived (the station is only about five blocks from my home).

I am thankful to have been born with the propensity to remain calm during emergencies. Yes, I do have emotions, but they only seem to set in once all the excitement is over. It is just a "mode" that I go into automatically – it requires absolutely no effort on my part to achieve. People sometimes find it strange or think that I am unemotional or uncaring. Not true at all. From a logical standpoint, screaming, worrying, and acting frantic and erratic are counter-productive behaviors in an emergency and do nothing to increase chances of survival. There's plenty of time for freaking out once the threat has passed. But it really isn't a matter of logic for me... it just happens.

So with my brain now in survival mode, I walked myself out to the ambulance, being sure to lock my door behind me. The crew was just pulling the gurney out of the back and saw that I was a bit unsteady. They told me to stop, that they'd come to me. Did I listen? Nope. It was embarrassing enough that they were in front of my house with their lights flashing... my neighbors might be watching! I actually just wanted to climb up into the ambulance myself (so maybe I should have called a cab, instead!), but they made me lie down on the gurney, strapped me down, and then loaded me in like a pallet of freight. To this day, I have no idea if any of my neighbors were home and watching. I sure hope not!

I must say that, by the time the doors slammed shut and we pulled out from in front of my house, my symptoms were well on their way to resolving on their own, and then I began to seriously rethink my decision to call 911. In my mind, I was rationalizing that what I had just been through was just a TIA (transient ischemic attack) or maybe even a migraine (as some migraines can present with stroke-like symptoms). The EMTs were radioing my information in to the hospital as we pulled away, and through the rear window, I could see a police officer checking out my house. Boy, I *hope* I locked the door like I thought I did – it was a real mess inside! The ambulance trip itself was not very exciting... not even a siren. I guess there wasn't enough traffic at that time of day. The EMTs tried starting IVs in both of my arms and in both of my hands with very little success. The bumpy ride alone would have made it hard enough for them, but that along with my "wiggly" veins must have made it nearly impossible. I felt like a pincushion.

In just a few minutes, we arrive at the hospital (it's less than three miles from my house). Wow, the scene there was quite impressive. The trauma center's stroke response team was waiting outside as we backed in like a semi to a loading dock. They had actually flung the ambulance doors open before we even came to a stop. I was almost expecting a forklift, but two of the crew yanked me out, pallet and all, and wheeled me into a small nearby triage room where they did a cursory check of my vitals, drew blood, etc. In the next moment, I was rushed off to radiology for a head CT to determine if the event was ischemic (a clot) or hemorrhagic (a bleed) in nature. I was so caught up in the flurry of activity and the precision and speed with which everyone on the team performed their roles that I actually forgot that I might be in very serious condition.

I was pretty sure that this event was not hemorrhagic, as I had been taken off of warfarin after my "successful" PVI and was now only on aspirin, fish oil, garlic oil, and vitamin E (both my CHADS2 and CHA2DS2-VASc scores were zero, so my EP thought it was OK to let me slide when I resisted his suggestion that I go back on warfarin). But as I thought about it, how could I even have an ischemic event being on all of those things? Well, I would later learn that aspirin is an antiplatelet, not an anticoagulant, and that platelets play no part in clots that form during a-fib (see Figure 4, page 254). So the aspirin that I had been taking offered no protection, whatsoever. And the other supplements, while they may help prevent clots from entering circulation, they are not anticoagulants, either, and do nothing to prevent clots from forming. So I guess I had been living in a fool's paradise.

Good news, though... my brain checked out OK. The team delivered me to a room in the ER where a neurologist was standing by to evaluate me. She looked over my history, asked me some questions about my symptoms, and checked my sensory and motor functions bilaterally. Everything seemed OK. I still had some dizziness, but I didn't know if it was from the recent event or just from my ongoing sinus issues. I also thought that I might have had slightly blurred vision, but I wasn't entirely sure. Still, the neurologist recommended that I take a shot of tPA (tissue plasminogen activator) just to be safe – if the event were caused by a clot from my recent bout of flutter, there may have been more clots waiting to break free. Made sense. She told me that, because the tPA will break down every clot anywhere in the body, there is a high risk of severe, possibly <u>fatal</u>, internal bleeding, especially if the patient has GI erosion or other internal damage. That didn't sound like fun. So I told her about my GERD and asked her what she would do in my shoes. She said that she'd take the shot. I would be admitted and closely monitored afterward, so even if there were a problem, I was in the very best place for it to happen. I gave her the thumbs-up and got a stack of papers in return (yes, it did occur to me that I may have been <u>literally</u> signing my life away). Then I got the shot. My fingers? They were crossed!

This tPA was the most amazing thing that I had ever witnessed. I already knew what it was like for my blood to clot slowly from my warfarin days, but this was much different. The instant the tPA was injected into my IV, blood began seeping from all breaches in my skin – from all the holes where the EMTs had stuck me during my ambulance ride, from the site where blood was drawn when I first arrived at the hospital, and from other miscellaneous cuts and scrapes on my hands and arms that had long since healed (or so I thought!). Blood even began seeping out from around my IV site. Fascinating! But my fascination turned to dread (OK, maybe just dismay) when the nurse took to taping gauze pads over each and every offending spot on both of my hairy arms to stem the flow of blood. I sure was not looking forward to ripping them off later!

When the bleeding finally stopped after a few hours, I was taken up to the ICU for the requisite 24 hours of post-tPA monitoring. In the ICU, I saw lots of familiar faces from my post-ablation stay just a little more than one year prior. But there was one nurse who seemed most familiar. Or at least he acted that way. He came over and talked to me as soon as he saw me, and it seemed like we were somehow old friends. He was definitely not one of my nurses from my previous visit, and I don't think that I had even seen him in there that time. It wasn't until much later, long after I was transferred out of the ICU, and maybe even after I left the hospital altogether, that I realized where I remembered him from – he was one of my mother's nurses while she was recovering from surgery almost six years earlier. I had seen him many times while visiting my mother and had discussed football and our tree house man cave with him on several occasions. I wonder if he ever remembered where he knew me from.

After that brief social interlude, I arrived at my room. My evening nurse, waiting with clipboard in hand, could have easily passed for a high schooler. Of course, as I creep up on the big Five-O (and not the "Hawaii" kind), I find that most younger people are starting to look that way to me. She really was very young, though, and I got the impression that she was new to the whole nursing gig because she seemed very meticulous, thorough, and "by the book". Fortunately, though, she was also very upbeat and friendly – I have had pretty good luck in this respect (of course these are ICU nurses – much different from the nurses that dwell amongst the general population). So we went over my medical history in great detail, and then she promptly conducted the first of what would be *many* rounds of the hospital's standard "stroke tests" – specific positioning and motions with each arm and then each leg, reading a list of words out loud, smiling, raising my eyebrows... you get the idea. These were to test for any worsening deficits that might be caused by bleeding in the brain (as a result of the tPA). I passed the tests, and because I was starving by this time, I asked if I could be rewarded (like a smart chimp) with some food. It was too late to have food services bring anything, but my most awesome nurse went on a mission and found some snack crackers and a soda for me. It was better than nothing... and probably better than any hospital meal that I would have received, anyway!

I don't think this nurse was accustomed to having a healthy patient in the ICU, or even a lucid patient. She spent much of her time hanging out in my room conversing with me rather than manning her assigned post just outside. Maybe she felt sorry for me because I complained (repeatedly!) about being so bored, but it really just seemed like a conversant patient was a welcome change for her. And it sure doesn't take much to get me talking. It started with her asking me details about my arrhythmia and ablation experiences (all the medical professionals seem fascinated with those details... maybe I should send them all copies of this book!), but then the conversations took crazy detours onto completely unrelated topics such as football, her brother, and her fiancée and their wedding plans. It, somehow, came up that her father's name was also Kevin and that he was the same age as me (definitely one of those "feeling old" moments). And I learned that he had once owned and operated a restaurant that I had considered possibly taking over just a few years earlier. Small world!

We had gone off on one particularly wild tangent that led to her story about a student teaching job that her brother had taken. (This is the kind of story that you don't forget, and possibly the highlight of this trip to the hospital, so I feel compelled to share it with you.) During one day on this student teaching job in a rural school district, my nurse's brother was in charge of the class, and the teacher was supposed to be observing and evaluating him. The teacher arrived late that day with a large paper bag in her hand and sat at a desk way in the back of the room. She proceeded to pull a dead, bloated raccoon carcass that she had picked up along the road on her way in to school that morning from the bag, retrieved a rusty, old butcher knife that she kept in her desk drawer (for just such an occasion?), and began "dissecting" this very ripe raccoon. Right there on the desk.

In the classroom. This was not only very distracting to her brother as he tried to teach, but the overwhelmingly foul odor also made many of the students sick. No kidding!

My nurse was laughing so hard telling this story (in much more gory detail, of course) that she could hardly finish it. It gave me a good laugh, too, and I have retold it to many others since then. Of course, all of this socializing was periodically interrupted by the requisite "stroke test" that would have to be repeated every hour during my stay. And it wasn't long before I had all of it memorized – all the movements and all the words. I really *was* a smart chimp! The nurses found it entertaining, too (they were periodically called in from neighboring rooms to watch my performance). I think that they might have actually been laughing *at* me, though, not *with* me... just the feeling that I got. Although, I did get one nice compliment during my stay – an older nurse who I hadn't even met stopped in as she walked by to tell me that I had a very soothing voice and that it was nice to hear me talking and laughing in a place that is normally so full of misery and stress. So that made me feel pretty good.

And then, it was the next day... April 23rd. I was to be released from the ICU either later this day or early the next day and relocated to the stroke ward. But as you know by having read this far, things are never that straightforward for me. My atrial flutter started up again. It wasn't insanely fast, in the 160s, I believe. The nurse called my EP (he was not even aware of my recent "event" yet). He discontinued the oral dronedarone and started, you guessed it, IV amiodarone. He had been trying to avoid this because of the toxic effects that it had been having on my body. I really wanted to avoid it, too, but I guess it was better than the alternative. He also started me on oral warfarin and IV heparin now that the tPA had cleared my system. And with these drugs came regular blood tests – along with the stroke tests that I still had to perform like clockwork every few hours. I spent that night in the ICU again and enjoyed more "funny story time" with my favorite nurse. She wasn't quite as jovial this time, though, distracted by my fast heart rate.

The next morning I was still in flutter, but I was otherwise too healthy to continue taking up valuable space in the ICU. So it wasn't long before they shipped me off to the stroke ward. More very young nurses, but not quite as friendly. And understandably so – the stress level in that wing was unbelievably high. Some of the patients that I saw the nurses helping to "walk" down the hall were very sad cases. It wasn't until I moved into this wing of the hospital that I realized just how lucky I had actually been. The stroke testing continued there, too, and these nurses were amused that I knew the whole routine by rote, too. And just as in the ICU, I was by far the most healthy and lucid patient there – and now by an even greater margin. My room was a semi-private, but I had no roommate during my stay, so again, it became the hang-out spot for many of the nurses and other staff members. If only I had been this popular in college!

I was only in my new room in the stroke ward for a few hours when, right after eating a very late lunch, I got a severe dizzy spell and felt a weird vibrating sensation in my gut. I rang for the nurse. My blood pressure was up. She checked my blood sugar... it was 159, a little high. She looked very concerned and did not want to waste any time, just in case. Stroke ward protocol was "when in doubt, MRI." She made a quick call down to radiology to make sure they could squeeze me in, and they told her to bring me right down. She found someone to cover for her in the ward and then took me down there herself. There was a one-patient wait when we arrived, so I was "parked" in the hall just outside the MRI room. My nurse stayed with me, making small talk, trying to keep me calm. I wasn't nearly as nervous as she seemed to be, but the look of concern on her face sure didn't put my mind at ease, either!

The assembly line was in motion, and when the person in front of me was rolled out of that workstation, I was rolled in. Wow, I guess they have to keep the MRI machine cool so it functions properly, but it was like a meat locker in that room! The techs, who were seemingly oblivious to the arctic conditions, connected my IV to the syringes of contrast agent in the remote injector mechanism, stacked what looked like irregular pieces of old carpet padding and used packing materials (hospital budgetary issues, perhaps?) on the machine's moving table, and asked me to lie down on them. The table was advanced into the tube to check the "fit" and then pulled right back out so that they could make adjustments to the padding. I had never had an MRI before but always figured that it would be pretty easy. Well, after just being in the tube for those few seconds, I could tell that it was going to be a far from enjoyable experience for me.

I have never been claustrophobic, but I do not like being restrained. Inside the MRI tube, I was pressed so tightly upward against the inside that I could not move anything. They told me that the test would take about 40 minutes, and they gave me a pneumatic rubber bulb to squeeze if I needed to get out. I was determined not to use that bulb no matter what. I figured that I've been through worse, so I should be able to get through this. They clamped my head down with a padded plastic frame, and in I went again. But once in position, there was so much force against my chest that I could hardly breathe. I yelled out, "This isn't going to work!" So they pulled me out again, removed the last bit of padding from underneath me, and replaced it with a thin, folded blanket, and then sent me back into the cold tube of doom one last time. It was very loud and extremely stressful. The stress was so great that, after only a few minutes, my ever so stubborn atrial flutter converted (my nurse noticed right away on the pulse-ox meter). That was the only positive thing that I could take away from that experience, that's for sure.

After that little field trip was over, I went back to my room where I would have to stay for a then indeterminate amount of time until my INR was in therapeutic range. This turned out to be about five days. Five long days! Fortunately, I had TV to pass some of the time, and of course, there were the nurses that liked hanging with me. And as a bonus, there was an older, motherly staffer (I don't think she was a nurse) who worked in the ward in the evenings and smuggled milk and "homemade" graham crackers with peanut butter to me every night. She even brought ice cream on one occasion! These "good times" were few and far between, though, relative to the ongoing regular stroke tests, blood tests, and unexpected harvesting of stool specimens (I guess someone was doing their homework and saw the investigative EGD the year before in my file and wanted to check for a GI bleed).

Lots of doctors visited me in the stroke ward, too. My EP was out of town that week, so several of his colleagues visited in his stead. The first to stop by was also the first cardiologist that I had seen after my a-fib started. He looked at my chart and asked me how I handled the MRI. I gave him the same account that I just gave you, and he told me his own personal story of "freaking out" in the machine. He absolutely could not do it, but he really needed this MRI, so he tried an open MRI machine. He described the open MRI as like lying on a slab the size of a bed and having another slab the size of a bed lowered down on top of you. He said that he freaked out in that one, too, so he ultimately needed to have it done under sedation. I felt a little less foolish for having a hard time with mine after hearing his story.

Later in the week, I was visited by another one of my EP's colleagues. This time, it was the doctor who performed the TEE prior to my ablation (the bad TEE). Was I on an episode of "This is Your Life"? And he remembered me, too – the guy who wouldn't go to sleep! I gave him a half-serious attitude about him torturing me while I was still conscious, but he said what could he do... he had a schedule to keep and my ablation was first thing the next morning. He was also only half-serious, too, but with a very deadpan style of delivery. What he said was true, though – he had other patients, and my procedure the next day depended, at least in part, on that TEE being completed. That was pretty much all we talked about, and then he left... I'm still not sure why he even stopped by. Maybe that was his way of evaluating me.

One of the other doctors that visited was the neurologist who had originally admitted me from the ER. She came to give me the report on my MRI/MRA (*Figure 5, page 255*). Besides some incidental findings – an arachnoid cyst on my right parietal lobe, a deviated nasal septum, and a large mucus retention cyst in my right maxillary sinus – there was evidence of a tiny infarct (area of dead tissue) in my right thalamus (a central structure in the brain that processes sensory input). It measured only about ½mm across, which equates roughly to a few thousand brain cells... DEAD! To put that into perspective, though, the human brain is made up of about 100 billion neurons, so this event claimed only about 0.000003% of my brain. That is hardly significant at all, especially considering that you can lose many more brain cells than this from a single night of heavy drinking. But because those brain cells lost to alcohol are typically distributed randomly throughout the brain, the effects are not immediately noticeable like they are when that same amount of damage is concentrated in one small isolated functional area of the brain, as happens with a stroke.

After the neurologist left and I reread the report a couple of times, I placed a call to what I felt was the leading local ENT practice and made an appointment to discuss the sinus cyst as well as the dizziness that I had been experiencing in recent months with one of their doctors. Then a gastroenterologist came in a little later to tell me that there was no blood found in my stool. And a hospitalist also came in to talk to me. Why, I am still not sure. I am not even sure what a hospitalist is or does. We had a very strange (mostly one-sided) conversation, which focused mainly on how important his function was, how impressive his qualifications were, and how very significant he was in the big scheme of things around the hospital... and I had absolutely no clue what he was talking about! He was pushy and rude, and he couldn't have left soon enough for me. Good riddance.

I was finally released from the hospital on the afternoon of April 27th when my INR stabilized in therapeutic range. I had prescriptions for amiodarone and warfarin in my discharge packet. Not a surprise. Even though I did not want to have to go back on either of these drugs, I accepted the fact that I would have to, at least for a little while longer. The warfarin, obviously, was to minimize the chance of having another one of these events. And the amiodarone was to keep me in NSR – it was the only thing that had ever worked for me, and even though the side effects were bad, a stroke could be much worse. But I already had made up my mind that I was going to seek out another surgical option right away so I could get off of these dangerous medications as soon as possible.

Moving forward, the amiodarone worked great, as I knew it would. It allowed only two short bouts of a-fib in May (each one lasting less than half an hour), none at all in June, and only, one more short bout in July. Then smooth NSR sailing from that point on. I was less than thrilled to think that I'd have to go to the Coumadin® Clinic once a week (or more!) again to get my INR tested, but then at my first visit (as if they read my mind), I was given the option to apply for home INR testing. Normally, this offer is only extended after the first 90 days on warfarin, but since I had been on it once before and for well over 90 days (before and after my ablation), I was already qualified. Finally, some luck.

I signed up for the home testing without hesitation, and the testing company and my insurance carrier both approved my application without any problems. I received my meter and a brief training session a few weeks later. It was very simple (because I had seen it done so many times before!). Testing at home, once a week, was so much more convenient than having to drive to the clinic, sign in, fill out the insurance forms, wait in the waiting room, get questioned by the tech, sign another form, get tested, wait for the results, and then wait for my new dosing instructions before driving back home. It was cheaper, too, and it afforded me the opportunity to test more frequently and devise a custom regulation scheme that kept my INR much more stable than the scheme that the clinic used (hmm... the subject of yet another book?).

Also in May, I had my initial visit with the ENT for my dizziness and the sinus cyst that was revealed by my MRI. He examined me and pulled up my recent imaging from the hospital's computer system, and besides the deviated nasal septum and that cyst in my sinus, he found nothing remarkable. So he ordered a whole laundry list of tests that would span the next two months – a hearing and ear pressure test with an audiologist, allergy tests, a sinus CT, a visual tracking test, a postprandial blood sugar test, and the Epley maneuver. The audiologist found normal middle ear pressure and only a slight high-frequency hearing loss consistent with my age group. And the allergy test showed that I was allergic to nothing at all, even though I still suffered from nasal and skin allergy symptoms to all the things that I had always been allergic to. The discrepancy may have been because of the beta blocker that I was on, but I never bothered to have the test redone without the beta blocker... I already knew what I was allergic to.

The sinus CT showed the same deviated septum and the same cyst that were shown on both the CT and the MRI that I had while in the hospital, but nothing more. The visual tracking test checked for visual or neurological problems that could affect balance. Part of this test uses warm air blown into one ear at a time while tracking eye motion with a laser as you try to stare at a stationary dot. It causes a severe spinning sensation, one direction when the air is blown into one ear, and then the opposite direction for the other ear. My body passed this test, too. The postprandial blood sugar test (performed two hours after eating) read 84... perfectly normal. Finally, the Epley maneuver – the patient lies on a table, head lower than feet, and his/her head is manipulated into various unnatural positions and held in each for about 15 minutes. It is designed to allow calcium deposits (called "otoconia") that form in the vestibular system to move to and settle in the ends of the semicircular canals where they are no longer able to contact nerve endings and interfere with balance. If the dizziness goes away after this procedure, then the doctor knows that the otoconia were the problem. Mine did not go away, so it was still a mystery.

Ultimately, the doctor told me to stop using the neti pot because it can irritate the mucus membranes in the sinuses and nasal passages and may cause a "rebound" effect. He said the same thing about the hot steam and essential oils that I had been using, too, and told me that they can actually make congestion worse. He gave me a prescription for, and a sample of, one of the steroid nasal sprays. I tried the spray and was very happy with its decongestant properties, especially since I hadn't used stimulant-based decongestant products for almost four years at this point. When I went to get the prescription filled, however, I was shocked to learn that it cost over $100 for a tiny one-month supply bottle... and that was *after* my insurance paid its part!

So I went back to the doctor and procured some more samples and three new prescriptions for similar steroid sprays that were also available. But when I checked each one at the pharmacy, they were all over $100. The spray worked great, but it wasn't worth $1,200/year to me. So I made the most of my samples by halving the dose and using it only as needed. And then I found out that a friend had a few bottles lying around that she wasn't using. I was able to make them last until just recently. And now one of the sprays has finally became available over the counter... for one-tenth the price! With continued use of this spray, the dizziness has slowly decreased. I still experience some from time to time, but not nearly as severe. The doctor also felt that removing the large cyst in my sinus might help some, but he wouldn't do the surgery until I was off the warfarin for good.

That May was really busy for me – I also had a follow-up appointment with the same neurologist who treated me in the hospital. We didn't really have much to discuss, and she hadn't ordered any follow-up tests because my symptoms had resolved with no lasting deficits (except the dizziness, which was not conclusively a result of my cerebrovascular event). My blood pressure was very high at this visit, but she thought that might be due in part to the anxiety attacks that I told her I was now having. She also asked about my sleep patterns, and I told her that I have never slept well, and that now I have been sleeping even less. She told me that a lack of sleep is a major cause of high blood pressure and can cause weight gain, and she wanted me to try Ambien. I never filled that prescription, though, because I had already had a history of sleepwalking, which up to that point had been harmless... and I wanted it to stay that way! Last, she told me that, after looking over my file, she noticed that none of my doctors had ever checked my T4 level along with my TSH level. She said that a TSH reading alone tells you nothing about the thyroid and that a free T4 reading is needed along with TSH to get a more complete and accurate picture of the thyroid's function. OK, I'd be sure to remember that.

My most important May follow-up, of course, was the one with my EP. And the most important part of that visit was our discussion about the convergent ex-maze procedure. It was relatively new, and very new to him and to my hospital. He told me that he was quite skeptical about the benefits of this new procedure over a regular PVI when his cardio-thoracic surgeon friend first approached him with the idea to start performing it. My EP, after all, had spent many years studying and performing the PVI for a-fib, and he truly believed in its great potential for positive patient outcomes. But after performing the first few of these ex-maze procedures, he became a believer. The outcomes were all positive with great success rates – especially among the most difficult to treat class of cases – and with minimal risk, complications, and recovery time similar to the catheter ablation that he had been so accustomed to performing.

In fact, this ex-maze procedure is basically just a catheter ablation, except it is performed on the outside of the heart, or "epicardially", as well as on the inside of the heart, or "endocardially", and creates a far more complex pattern of more complete lesions than the PVI (*see Figure 2b, page 252* – this is an example of the basic lesions, each type of procedure has its own unique set). It is one of several so-called "mini-maze" procedures – or minimally-invasive versions of the original Cox "cut and sew" maze procedure.

The Cox procedure entailed putting the patient on a heart bypass machine, opening the chest, stopping the heart, making calculated slices through the heart muscle, and then stitching it all back together, causing scar tissue to form that will eventually block the signals that cause a-fib. The mini-maze procedures do not require opening the chest and are performed while the heart is still beating, just like an ablation. Some of these procedures are performed thoracoscopically and require that one or both lungs be collapsed to gain the necessary access to the rear of the heart where the bulk of the work is performed, but the ex-maze avoids this additional risk. It is performed trans-diaphragmatically via a pericardioscope inserted through a small upper-abdominal incision, reducing the chance for complications and shortening recovery time.

After researching them all, I was sold on this new procedure. And I liked that I could have it done at my local hospital with an EP who I already knew, liked, and trusted. So I visited with the cardiothoracic surgeon who partnered with my EP on the ex-maze, and he discussed with me his part of the procedure and showed me the actual equipment that he and his team would use. After a brief hands-on demonstration on a model heart (gotta love the visual aids!), I was even more convinced that this was the right procedure for me. I liked what I saw, and I was very excited to get on with it. I may have been too excited, though, because at that point I think he might have suspected that I was a bit mentally unstable. He stressed to me that this was major surgery and that it was not to be taken lightly. Just because I was smiling and happy didn't mean that I was oblivious to the risks. Honestly, though, the risks that he described seemed low (similar to an ablation) and they were especially minimal when compared to suffering from another, possibly worse, stroke or even to the long-term damage that a lifetime of taking amiodarone and warfarin might do. So I said, "Sign me up!" There was already a long waiting list for the ex-maze at my hospital... people from all over the country! The soonest they could get me on the schedule was November 8th, and believe me, it could not come quick enough!

Over the coming months, I would still suffer from sudden, unexpected anxiety attacks – the only real lasting effect of the stroke – and I expended a great deal of mental effort to overcome them. It was quite a struggle at times, and it often seemed like my efforts were in vain. But in the end, I did overcome it. It was a rough four or five months, but I did it without the use of the mind-altering, potentially-addictive medications that several doctors had offered to me (even tried to "push" on me, on several occasions). I can understand how those drugs may be necessary to some who do not have the luxury of time needed to do it on their own, but taking them really does not strengthen or empower a person. In my opinion, by only masking your fears and shielding you from reality, these drugs only serve to weaken you and trap you in a cycle of dependency. Being already *physically* weakened by my heart arrhythmias, I could not afford to be mentally weakened on top of that. I needed to hang on to some shred of fortitude in my life so I could get myself back to normal (or as close to it as possible) in preparation for enduring and recovering from the big event that was awaiting on the horizon.

So I pushed myself to return to a more or less normal life. Especially difficult for me was taking trips away from home – my anxiety level was quite high, at first. But repeatedly putting myself in those types of situations that made me face that anxiety forced me to overcome it. It seemed like it took forever, and I am surprised that I had the patience for it, but I finally began to feel good again. On my own. No drugs. What also helped me to feel better – both physically and emotionally better – was that, without even trying and after plateauing about eight months earlier, a good deal more of the weight that I had gained during the first two years of my a-fib had finally started to come off again. Now all that I needed to feel really good was to get off of the amiodarone and the warfarin. That was my goal, anyway. And that is when I'd know that my mission was complete. Every day that I was able to hang in there and move forward was one more day closer to that goal.

Renewed Hope –
The Ex-Maze

It had been an eternity since my last doctor visit, and the uphill battle that I fought against my post-stroke anxiety made it seem even longer. But November was finally here. Summer and half of autumn had already come and gone with but a few notable highlights. I finished and published the band's first CD – the official release was set for August, so we had a hard deadline to meet. The release party was an all-day outdoor bash featuring several musical acts, and yours truly was sound man for all of them. I also assisted with another multi-band outdoor gig and took part in the ritualistic annual repair of our tree house in preparation for the approaching football season. And with my surgery just around the corner, the sudden tragic illness and passing of my friends' beloved pet brought unwelcome grief. Everyday stuff, but all the while I was still living under the cloud of amiodarone and warfarin – the last two monkeys on my back.

In just a few days, though, I was about to undergo the convergent ex-maze procedure to (hopefully) put an end to my atrial fibrillation and atrial flutter. And even though it would be quite a bit more involved and more serious than the ablation that I had had almost two years earlier, I didn't have any of the nerves in the weeks leading up to it like I did before the ablation. Maybe it had something to do with being preoccupied by my mother's recovery from back-to-back cataract surgeries just weeks earlier. Or maybe it was the rush to tie up loose ends with my clients before my indeterminate period of down time. It could also have been the weeks of incessant house cleaning that I did to prepare for potential helplessness while recovering from this surgery (I always try to be prepared for every eventuality!) In any case, the only emotion that I felt at that point was the excitement that the time had finally come.

Monday, November 7, 2011: Procedures had changed a little since my last visit to the EP lab. This time I was to report to the Coumadin® Clinic on the morning of my admission for an INR test and then to my cardiology group's imaging center to have the cardiac CT done (this is what the EP would use to navigate during the next day's procedure). After the scan, I was given a CD with the imaging data on it to take with me to the hospital later that day. One of my biggest regrets to this day is that I did not make myself a copy of this disc when I stopped at home to pick up my things before going to the hospital. Who knows if I could have even viewed the files on my home computer... but it would have been fun to try!

I arrive at the hospital later that day (about mid-afternoon) for the standard hospital admissions rigmarole that I had now been through too many times. But this time, I was not taken to a regular room amongst the general population after admissions. Instead, I was held in a berth in the prep room just across the hall from the EP lab. I wasn't there long, though, before being wheeled away for a TEE. I specifically requested propafol for my TEE when had I signed up for the ex-maze many months earlier, and my EP backed me up on it considering the bad experience that I had had before my PVI. I just hoped that the orders made it onto whatever paperwork the hospital had on file for me that day. But my fears were quickly allayed when I saw that the anesthesiology team was already there in the procedure room when I arrived. That could have only meant one thing... propafol!

So this time the TEE went off without a hitch, and when I awoke, I was back in my stall in the EP lab's prep room. I did *not* have an unbearable sore throat or severely strained chest and abdominal muscles like I did after my previous TEE, thankfully. I noticed that some IVs had been started during my brief hiatus from consciousness, and as soon as my lucidity was detected, the staff converged upon my stall. I was in for a rude awakening, indeed... it was time to be shorn. Baaa! I was not even offered the option of doing it myself as I had been for my first procedure, but the nurse that was charged with this unpleasant task performed it with the utmost respect for my privacy and managed to deflect the awkwardness of the situation with some idle chatter.

When the deed was done, I was asked to vacate the premises while what seemed like the entire housekeeping crew was brought in, Shop-Vac® in tow, with a complete set of fresh bed linens. No, nothing embarrassing about that.

When I was finally allowed to settle in for the evening, I watched some TV (what else is there to do?) until dinner arrived. I ate, and then I watched even more TV. I was beginning to regret leaving my laptop at home, and I really missed the friendly nurses of the ICU and stroke ward. Even though I am not a huge football fan, ever since building the tree house – the "Eagles Nest" – with my friends and watching most of the Philadelphia Eagles® games up there with them, I had now felt compelled to follow the team. They were playing the Chicago Bears® that night, and although the Eagles lost, it was a good way to pass the time... and I would be up to speed for the next time that I talked to my friends. I could hear that at least a few other people in the prep room had also stayed up to watch the game. As the Bears' lead grew, though, I heard one and then the next TV switching off around me. Good idea... I'd better get some sleep for the long arduous day tomorrow.

Tuesday, November 8th: I was awoken early to have blood drawn just before my breakfast arrived. Breakfast? Wow... the last time that I was in this situation, I was NPO after midnight on Sunday and didn't really eat anything until Wednesday afternoon, and I was starving and felt horrible. So having something to eat now was good, I thought... maybe I wouldn't feel so bad when I came out of surgery this time.

After enjoying my mediocre hospital food service breakfast, I washed up and then just walked across the hall to the EP lab. It was so much better than having to be carted in on a bed. To my surprise, a good number of the staff present that day remembered me from my previous visit. But you never know if they just saw in my file that I was there before and were only trying to put me at ease, so I had to ask them if it was just an act or if they really did remember me. They said that I stood out because I was cheerful and talkative – not the norm for most people about to undergo a serious heart procedure. They said that most of the patients they see are scared and sick or already sedated. So I guess it's good to be a little strange sometimes. Score one for mental instability!

The greatest benefit of walking into the EP lab instead of rolling in on a bed was that I could take a little stroll. OK, maybe I was just putting off the inevitable, but I also wanted to "see the sights" this time. I got the feeling that the staff wasn't thrilled with my self-guided tour, but they let it slide. I guess it was my good rapport with them. Besides, it was only a minute, and I sure wasn't going to mess with anything because my life would depend on it over the next few hours! My walk-through really gave me a better feel, though, for the size of the room, the size the crew, and the amount of equipment used. Of course, this being a far more serious procedure than my PVI, there were additional equipment and staff – most noticeable was the cardiothoracic team on stand-by with a cardiopulmonary bypass machine... "just in case". Let's hope we won't be needing either of them today!

There was a schedule to keep, unfortunately, and I couldn't stall any longer, so I took my familiar spot on the table. The prep team converged upon me, same as before. A few of them who remembered me had asked about how the first procedure had worked for me and how my health had been since then, so I gave them a brief update. I was surprised when one of them had commented about the weight that I had lost in the interim (some, but not nearly all of the 60 pounds that I had gained before the first procedure). I was also surprised that they were *not* shocked that my a-fib and flutter had returned. In fact, they said that they were quite used to seeing "repeat customers" for ablations. They seemed to be taken aback by the news of my cerebrovascular event, however, since I was relatively young and in good general health. But they reassured me that they have had great success with this ex-maze procedure that I was about to undergo. Yes, my EP and my cardiothoracic surgeon both had said the same thing... that's a big reason why I was there!

After being prepped in a similar fashion to when I was in for the PVI, the time to say goodnight was soon upon me. The ease with which I relinquish control in this situation (e.g., being knocked out for surgery or the like) surprises me – and not just this time but every time – given my typical resistance to releasing the reigns. I guess it is a "point of no return" type of thing. Naturally, the thought always crosses my mind that I may simply not wake up. I believe that's only natural. But it's never accompanied by fear. What better way to go, really? No pain. No suffering. Never aware that it has even happened. Of course, then everything leading up to this moment would be for naught... I certainly did not want that! I mean, there had to be a purpose to all that I had been through. Right? And as the anesthesia began to flow, I closed my eyes, looking forward to reopening them in the new realm of extreme discomfort that would inevitably follow.

And in the virtual blink of an eye, I began hearing voices and other sounds. Soon after, I was moving and able to open my eyes... I think I made it! And I didn't feel as bad as I had expected to. (Was it because I ate breakfast?) It appeared that I was in the ICU, a place that I knew all too well by this time. But that was OK, I knew that it was standard practice for this procedure. But as soon as I looked at the clock and saw the light level outside, I knew that something was wrong. It was only early in the afternoon. Of course, I did not know what day it was (or even what year, for that matter!), so it could have been even worse than I had imagined. Before my mind completely grasped the concept that I may have just awoken from a long coma, though, my nurse came in to check on me. She told me that there was a problem with the equipment during the procedure, and that they had to end it early. She said that my doctor would stop by to give me the details tomorrow. I really didn't know what to make of it because, even though I didn't feel quite as bad as the last time, I sure didn't feel good... I mean, I definitely felt like some sort of procedure had been performed on me!

As I became more lucid, I became more aware of the pain. Severe stabbing pain in my chest with every beat of my heart, extreme burning sensation in my chest with every breath, and least but still significant, pain from stitches (internal and external) in my upper abdomen whenever I tried to move. The procedure that I had just had (the convergent ex-maze) involved, in addition to endocardial radio frequency (RF) ablation similar to that performed in the PVI that I previously had, an incision just below the sternum and another incision through the diaphragm just in front of the esophagus (which, in turn, was made laparoscopically via two small incisions, one on each side beneath the ribcage) through which the pericardioscope was inserted. This gives the surgeon direct access to the rear of the heart, allowing a more complete RF ablation to be performed epicardially on parts of the heart muscle that cannot be reached from the inside.

The part of the procedure performed on the outside of the heart causes some bleeding and fluid buildup within the pericardium (pericardial effusion), and this fluid must be drained so it does not accumulate and exert pressure on the outside of the heart. To allow this blood to drain, a tube is snaked through the chest via one of the laparoscopy incisions, through the diaphragm, and left inserted in the pericardial sac after the procedure. Between the massive amount of irritation caused by the burns on the outside of the heart and the friction of this drainage tube rubbing against it, the pain was quite significant, to say the least, especially every time my heart moved (so about once every second!). It was this same tube running through my chest cavity that made breathing very painful and quite difficult. I was so distracted by these pains, that I didn't even remember that my femoral veins had been punctured until the nurse came in to check my groins.

I noticed that I wasn't quite flat on my back like I was forced to lie the last time. Everything else was pretty much the same, though – all the IVs, monitor leads, pulse ox sensor, blood pressure cuff, and leg cuffs tying me down to my bed. There was also an arterial line in my right wrist for blood pressure, just like before, but this time the immobilizing board was not strapped very securely to my arm and hand. This was particularly worrisome for me at night when I would try to sleep (remember my fear of bleeding out?). Oh, and I had the ever-so-pleasant Foley catheter again, too. Hourly chest x-rays, EKGs, echocardiograms (quite painful with an incision in the area of interest), and blood tests followed. And the oral meds began almost right away, too.

Dinner came, but I was still in a fog and I hadn't even thought about being hungry or if it was even time to eat. I sure didn't feel like eating between the pain and residual nausea from the anesthesia. The nurse came in to give me a shot of morphine for the pain without even asking if I needed it, and when I found out what it was, I turned it down. I had never had morphine before, and I had heard of people getting sick from it or having other bad reactions to it. I already felt a little sick and didn't want it getting worse. Plus I knew that morphine was addictive, so I felt like I would rather try to overcome the pain on my own. Well, that was much easier said than done with this pain! The nurse kept telling me that my doctor always orders morphine as a standard part of this procedure – 15mg every 4 hours. I think I was actually groaning, it hurt that bad. I'm sure I even had tears in my eyes. I laugh just thinking about it now because it seems like I was being silly, but it really did hurt... bad! So bad that it made me rethink everything else that I had ever experienced that I thought was pain. I finally broke down later in the evening and agreed to only a *half-dose* of the morphine. I figured it couldn't hurt to try it, and it would get the nurse off my back. If it made me sick, I'd stop it. Well, it worked great... really great! And fast! And it was enough to allow me to fall asleep that night.

Wednesday, November 9th: Another day just like the rest in the ICU, with the exception of a protocol for this procedure that I was heretofore unfamiliar with... the periodic so-called "stripping" of the drainage tube. It is much worse than it sounds. This is done to clear out any clotted blood or bits of tissue that may otherwise clog the tube. The nurse holds the tube stationary at the point where it comes out of the body with one hand while pinching and rapidly sliding her fingers down the length of the exposed tube toward the collection vessel with the other hand. This creates additional suction in the tube, sucking the open end of the tube that is inside your chest to whatever is nearby... most likely to something that is already raw, irritated, and highly sensitive from the surgery that you just had. This was **extremely** painful! And each time the nurse came in to do it, she did it several times.

And each time, it left me on the verge of shock. I soon began having anxiety every time the nurse even passed near my door. OK, not really, but now I am pretty sure that I know how it feels to have a dagger plunged through your heart.

This was the morning after "something went wrong", and my EP visited me as promised. He walked in with a sheepish look on his face, obviously not sure if I had heard the news yet. I told him that I knew that they couldn't finish the procedure, but I hadn't heard the details. Well, it seems that the cardio-thoracic surgeon worked through a few minor glitches with the fluoroscope and then finished his part of the procedure without any issues. My EP tested and verified all of the epicardial lesions that were made in the first part of the procedure, and then they powered down while my incision was closed up. When they fired up the fluoroscope again for part two of the procedure, the glitch was back. My EP noticed it, but then it seemed to go away, so he decided to proceed. Just a few minutes later, though, the fluoroscope went out altogether, and he had to call it quits until it could be repaired (that's what was happening today).

Yeah, that sounds about right, considering the luck that I had had up to this point. My EP went on to tell me that this equipment gets regular inspections and has *never* failed during a procedure before. In fact, he told me that he had never experienced any failure of any equipment on any of the procedures that he has ever performed in that EP lab (or in any EP lab, for that matter) and neither have any of his colleagues. I told him not to worry about it, that I was used to this kind of thing! Everywhere I go, I seem be involved in a "this has never happened to us before" type of situation. I am also the guy that gets the slice of cherry pie with the pit or the crab cake or scrambled eggs with the piece of shell.

Anyway, he said that the technician was working on the fluoroscope as we spoke, and that it should be up and running later in the day. He then presented me with the option to either go home the next day and come back in three months for the second (endocardial) part of the procedure or to stay and go back under tomorrow to finish up. I proposed to him that a better option would have been to bring me out of anesthesia during the procedure to let me have a look at the fluoroscope, and then perhaps we'd be done by now, and we wouldn't be having this conversation. He laughed and commented to the effect that he expected me to say something like that. I guess my "humor" (and I use the term loosely) is pretty predictable once you get to know me. But seriously, I told him, "I already feel like crap. Let's just get it over with tomorrow." I got the feeling that that was what he wanted to hear, and I knew that if I went home, I definitely would not have wanted to come back in three months. (I just couldn't go through all that shaving again!)

My mother called in a little later that day. She said that she had called in the day before and got word from the nurse that something had gone wrong with the equipment and that the procedure had to be stopped early, but she was only slightly concerned. So then I filled her in on the details. The rest of the day passed without incident. Boredom, TV, sleeping, eating. Tests, meds, stripping. Oh, and now a lung capacity test – blow into a tube to see how high you can get the ping pong ball to go. Quite an uncomfortable task with a garden hose coiled inside your chest. And when I complained of a bad headache that night, my nurse said that he could only give me acetaminophen. I am not sure why. Maybe a doctor's order. He offered me no reason at all for this edict. Having taken acetaminophen my whole life (thinking I was allergic to aspirin), I knew how little it did for me. Still, it was acetaminophen or nothing, and my nurse was almost insisting that I take it. Was he on commission?

When the shift changed and my overnight nurse came in, however, she wanted me to sleep for the big day tomorrow (part two of my surgery). But I just couldn't... maybe from already sleeping after the procedure or because of the bad headache that I still had. She saw that there was alprazolam (Xanax®) ordered for me in case I had anxiety (I guess over the chest pains), and she told me that it might also help me to sleep. I really didn't want to take it for the same reasons that I didn't want the morphine. But she persisted, so I gave it a try (again, figuring that it can't hurt). Again, it worked great! In about 15 minutes, I zonked out – I might have even slept better there in the hospital and in pain than I ever do at home! Might have to get me some of that there stuff to go.

Thursday, November 10th: A rude and most unceremonious awakening in the ICU (made even ruder by the fact that I was sleeping so soundly) with no breakfast and no bathing. I was just wheeled straight down to the EP lab. Everyone in the lab had that same sheepish look that my doctor had when he came in to talk to me the day before. I think it was actually pity. Pity for me having to go through it all again... twice in three days! But I am pretty tough, and I still had my eyes on the prize. And they didn't have to cut me again – that part was finished. I joked about the whole situation with the staff... what else could I do, really? At least the heart bypass machine and surgical team where not there this time! So as the crew slapped foil all over my body (again) and checked all my rubber pads still left on from part the first, I asked them to please not stop for anything this time because I really wanted to be home by Christmas! And with some light-hearted reassurances, the anesthesia flowed once again, and I was out like a faulty fluoroscope.

And then... I awoke. But did I? I wasn't sure if I was coming to while I was still being worked on or if I was experiencing the afterlife. I saw large shadowy blue figures looming over me, and it felt like they were still working on me. It seemed like it was dark, but I could somehow still see them. And they were talking, but not about me. Actually, I couldn't really make out what I thought that I was hearing, but I felt terrified, and I wasn't sure why. Soon I was in a panic, and I screamed "Help me!" over and over, but they didn't react. No one reacted. There was no response at all. And as my situation became ever more desperate my anesthesia continued to wear off, and I soon realized that I had been hallucinating. I guess that's what it was - not sure since I had never hallucinated before! Reality rushed in quickly then, and I began to realize just how bad I actually felt... much worse than any other time that I had ever had anesthesia. This was, I am guessing, because I was weakened by the first part of the procedure and had also just had general anesthesia twice in only three days.

I just left my eyes closed and tried to sleep it off. I may have actually fallen asleep for a short while, but I suddenly realized the sensation of liquid running down the inside of my legs. Blood! My femoral veins blew open, and now I was bleeding to death! My biggest fear, and it was actually happening. Well, in my mind it was. I called for help several times, but my voice was hoarse and weak from being intubated. My eyes were still closed, so I had no idea if anyone was around. I raised and waved my one semi-free arm. My nurse came in and asked me what was wrong, and I told him that I was bleeding from the groins. Help!

Well... don't call the cavalry just yet. It was just sweat! Seems like I was a bit overheated from the mountain of blankets that they left piled on top of me from the recovery room (the patient's body temp drops considerably during so many hours in the meat locker-like EP lab). And because it was November, the heat in the ICU was also on. Blankets *and* heat... a bad combination for me, even on a good day (but not nearly as bad as bleeding to death). They relieved me of some of the blankets, and as I cooled off, I finally opened my eyes. It was dark outside. I looked at the clock. It was evening. That seemed about right. My dinner had already arrived and was there waiting for me, in vain of course. I am sure that I was hungry since I hadn't eaten in almost 24 hours, but I felt very sick. There was just no way that I could eat. I think I had a few sips of soda, that was all.

The pain in my chest was now much better than it had been, though. Maybe lying motionless in one position and barely breathing for all those hours allowed it to heal some. The stripping was still extremely painful, and the breathing tests were also still very uncomfortable. I didn't have to lie completely flat right after the procedure this time – I guess they learned that it was not necessary in the two years that had passed since my PVI. My head was slightly elevated this time, and I could have the wedge pillow under my legs right from the get go. My back still hurt quite a bit just from lying flat on a hard cold table for so long, but after sipping a little more soda and watching lots of boring TV, I finally fell asleep.

Friday, November 11th: Yes, it was 11/11/11... my lucky day! Well, maybe not "lucky", exactly. But eleven *is* my favorite number. Why? I'm not really sure, but my affinity for it goes way back to the earliest memories of my childhood. Maybe it's because eleven rhymes with Kevin. Or maybe it's because I have always just happened to look at the clock when it reads (or sometimes just as it changes to) 11:11. Anyway, this was that day. The day that I had thought about for such a long time. No thoughts in particular, though, just thoughts of its eventual arrival and musings about what I might be doing when this glorious day came. And here it was. And here I was... in the hospital ICU after having heart surgery. Day one of my recovery – 11/11/11.

This is the day after the procedure, again (remember, this was part two of my so rudely interrupted surgery). I feel much better, again. Except this time my hands were very puffy. The rest of me probably was, too, but I could really only see my hands. I know that they give Lasix® (a powerful diuretic) during and after the procedure because of the huge amount of water that must be pumped through the catheter to keep the tip cool as it cooks the heart tissue. Maybe they didn't give me enough this time. I brought it to the nurse's attention, and he shot me up with some more. When he checked the Foley bag a little later, it was quite full – full of dark brown urine. I am no doctor, but I knew that that probably wasn't good. Then it occurred to me that the bad pain in my middle back might have been from my kidneys and not just from lying flat. I think the same thought crossed my nurse's mind, but he was new to working in the ICU, so he asked his "trainer" about it. She said that it was a normal reaction to the IV antibiotic that I was on. I was skeptical, but eventually my puffiness went down, and my urine returned to normal. So the subject was dropped and never reported to my doctor.

My afternoon nurse then told me that I was on track to be transferred to a regular room soon and that I could be discharged tomorrow (Saturday) but only if there was a doctor available to see me. If not, I would probably have to stay until Monday. Hey, the sooner I could get out of there, the better! So my nurse prepared me for my transfer by removing my Foley, a-line, and IVs, just like after my ablation (it was the same nurse, too, by the way, but no Spiderman effect this time). Oh, apparently, the hospital no longer required the hourly bladder ultrasound after being taken off the Foley catheter, either, because he did not perform a single one of them on me this time.

When my lunch arrived, I was very hungry (I hadn't eaten much breakfast that day), and I ate most of it. Within about 15 minutes, I began shaking and feeling dizzy, and my blood pressure went way up. It seemed to me like it might have been a blood sugar issue, but my nurse refused to check my blood sugar because I was not diaphoretic (sweaty). But I was still on the high dosage of beta blocker, which can suppress diaphoresis and mask high or low blood sugar. Still, my nurse wouldn't take the two minutes it takes to perform the test. This whole episode reminded me of that time six months earlier when the same thing had happened to me in the stroke ward. That time, though, the nurse *did* check my blood sugar, and it *was* high. But this time, who knows. It cleared up after a while, but I was sure to order the lowest-carb foods that they had on the menu for the rest of my stay.

The last two things that I had to wait for before I could be transferred were to have the chest drain tube removed and for someone from Physical Therapy to evaluate me and sign off on my release. My nurse didn't take me around for a walk to prepare me like he did after my ablation. He probably should have, but now that all my tubes and wires were disconnected, I was able to move between the bed and chair pretty easily whenever I wanted to. And I was also able to use the toilet in the corner of the room when necessary. So when the PT "inspector" arrived, I was fairly steady on my feet, and I got the OK to be transferred. One down, one to go!

It seemed like an eternity before a hospital tech finally arrived to pull out my drain tube. He was all business, a man of few words, little humor, and apparently no regard for patient comfort. He said, "It's time this thing comes out." He put on his gloves and face shield and ripped off the bandages. Then, pressing down hard around the incision with one hand, he grabbed the tube with the other hand and told me to take a deep breath. He counted, "one, two..." and then just yanked the tube out! It was the absolute worst pain that I have ever felt in my entire life. It was so bad that I think that I actually might have blacked out for a moment. But then the pain was gone in that very same moment, so I pulled through just fine. I couldn't believe how long the tube was. He said it was 60cm... that's two feet! No wonder it was causing me pain. I instantly felt so much better with it out of my chest. I could breathe without pain and could take full, deep breaths once again (as evidenced by my subsequent superior performance on the breathing machine).

As though that brief but excruciating moment was some sort of rite of passage, official word that I was being released from my fishbowl of room in the ICU immediately followed. I'd miss this room where I enjoyed the comfort of having a single nurse watching over me at all times. But it was also the room full of beeping equipment where I had been tied down by tubes and wires and with the constant, never-ending stream of technicians coming in to practice their trades on me... and a room with a fold-away toilet on the wall with nothing but a curtain around it. As a black-shirt minion came in to take me by wheel chair to my new, "regular" room (a room in a completely different building on the hospital campus), a brief wave of nostalgia overcame me... and then quickly passed. Ciao!

Somehow I lucked out and landed a large private room way down at the end of the hall, far away from the bustle and noise of the nurses' station, with a giant flat-panel TV on the wall and full digital cable (the ICU only had small TVs with just the basic channels)! This was the first time during this stay that I was really happy – I knew that I wouldn't miss the season premiere of one of my favorite cable network shows. And I could watch it undisturbed because, even though the vampires still came by regularly, I never saw a single nurse (not even one just walking past my room) except when it was time for my meds. The solitude and quiet of this particular private room was such a welcome change, and I never thought that I would be so happy just to have a bathroom with a door (even though I still had the heart monitor on and could not yet take a shower). But the staff that serviced the patients among the general population lived up to my expectations of being largely disagreeable and inattentive, with the single exception of the girl who delivered my meals... she was very friendly.

After polishing off a dinner that was as low-carb as I could build from the hospital food service menu, I watched lots of

TV until a nurse came in to give me my nighttime meds. She talked to me for a while about my whole hospital stay and the procedure that I had just undergone, but it wasn't a friendly kind of talk. It was more like a teacher talking to a student, as though she was trying to explain everything that I had been through. Uh, here's news, lady... I wouldn't have chosen to go through it if I hadn't already completely understood it! Then, true to form, when she came back a little while later and found that I was still awake, she scolded me. What did it matter to her? I had no plans for the next day, did I? I mean, it was a Saturday, and the hospital would basically be shut down (except for that one yet-to-be-identified doctor who would, fingers crossed, stop by to discharge me). Still, she wanted me to sleep and saw in my file that I had been given Xanax® two nights earlier. She asked if I would like another one to help me sleep again, and I took it without hesitation this time. It really did help me to sleep, just like before. Fifteen minutes, and I was out cold.

Saturday, November 12th: Just after breakfast, a general surgeon (coincidentally, an associate of the surgeon who performed my hernia repair) came in to give me a once-over. He pulled my bandages and checked my incisions, he looked over my chart, and then he gave his final OK for me to go home. There was much rejoicing! Thankfully, the checkout process was long enough for me to get one more delicious meal in before I left. And after lunch, I called my brother to come and get me. The parking garage was a long way away from my room, and since I was in a regular room on a regular floor, and since it was a Saturday, there was no one around to cart me out. That was fine by me. I found being wheeled around in a chair to be a bit demeaning anyway. So I walked... slowly but surely, and somewhat unsteadily. By the time I got to the garage, I was nearly exhausted. That was the most exercise that I had had over the last six days.

Back at home, I was hoping to be able to get back to normal quicker than I had after my ablation, so while I still took it easy as instructed, I did not just sit in bed for fear of popping open the puncture sites like I had done the first time around. I was stuck twice in each groin this time (because of the delay caused by the equipment failure), and I did still have some seepage from both sites. I had some pain, too, but this time I was an "old pro" (much like a mother with her second baby) and did not worry about anything. I still had to wait about another week for the scabs to start coming off of the incisions on my abdomen before I could take a shower, and I followed the discharge instructions as far as restrictions on driving, lifting, and going stairs. Overall, the healing process was quicker than after my PVI. The biggest problem was the *lack* of pain from the main central incision after only the first few days. This was a problem because I'd forget to prepare or take it easy whenever I had to cough or sneeze, but then when I did, the intense pain was sure to remind me! It was actually quite a while before I could cough, sneeze, or lift without some amount of pain. In fact, I still do have some slight pain at the site of the internal incision from time to time, nearly three years later.

At my three-week follow-up with the cardiothoracic surgeon who performed the epicardial portion of my ex-maze, I was 100% healed (externally, anyway) except for a single stitch that was sticking out of the scar from the main central incision. It was the cut end that stuck out of a knot. The knot had already scarred over (leaving a large hard lump, which I still have) but hadn't yet dissolved. The surgeon wiped the area with alcohol and then simply grabbed the stitch with a set of forceps, pulled it as taut as he could (this did not feel good) and snipped it flush with the skin with sterile surgical scissors. The process reminded me of the "lift and cut" razor blades that you see in TV commercials. When he cut the stitch, it retracted and disappeared. The hole scarred over quickly after that. I really could have just done that same thing myself at home... that one stitch had been bothering me for weeks!

Around this same time, I also had a follow-up with my EP who performed the endocardial portion of my ex-maze. His professional opinion... all was well. Yes, I was still having strange (very strange) arrhythmias from time to time, but the bouts were diminishing by the day. On January 14, 2012, I had my last protracted bout of chronic a-fib. Three days later, my EP ordered a 48-hour Holter monitor. It was almost a month ahead of schedule, but I think he was as anxious to get me off of the amiodarone as I was to get off of it. I had only two more very short bouts of a-fib spaced about six weeks apart before my next scheduled follow up appointment on April 21st. That is when I officially got the good news – the Holter results from January were good, and since it was now five months post-op, it was time to stop the amiodarone. I had been on it exactly one day short of one full year this time. My EP didn't seem to think anything of the two short bouts of a-fib spaced so far apart, but he did want me to come in for another follow-up in just two months to see how I was after stopping the antiarrhythmic.

One week *after* stopping the amiodarone, I received an order for the standard battery of blood tests used to monitor the side-effects of this highly toxic drug – I had submitted to these tests numerous times already, but I obviously did not need them any more. Some of the individual tests included in the order, though, were of interest to me. So I went to the lab with the order and simply refused (crossed off with a black marker) the tests that I did not find necessary. The lab personnel didn't seem to care. After all, I should have the right to choose what I wish to pay for. Right? Well, when the cardiology office received the results and saw that certain tests that they had ordered were not performed, I got a call. I told them that that my EP stopped my amiodarone at my last visit and that the tests that I refused were no longer necessary. Besides, I should not have even received the order for these tests at all, I told them. They got very indignant with me and told me that that was not for me to decide. Wrong! If it is my money, then it is my decision. Oh well, it wouldn't be the first time that I have done something that upset someone. I figured they'd eventually get over it... or they wouldn't. Who cares either way.

Before my June follow-up with my EP, I had one more short bout of a-fib. This came about six weeks after the previous short bout, just like before. During this visit I was in NSR, but I told my EP about the recent bout of a-fib, and he considered it to be very insignificant compared to the severity of my bouts prior to the surgery (as did I!), and he said that he was comfortable declaring the procedure a success at that time. Great news! And even more great news... he said that, *if it were up to him*, he'd stop the warfarin in three months, too, as long as I remained in NSR. To be off both drugs – a dream come true. I couldn't wait!

But then he said that it wouldn't be up to him. I guess with every piece of good news there always has to be some not-so-good news to balance it out – seems that way, anyway. My EP told me that he would be leaving the practice – leaving the state, in fact – in August. He was relocating for personal reasons, and he would be joining the faculty of a university medical school in his new home town and would become the director of complex cardiac ablation at their hospital, gracing others whose lives have been put on hold by this disorder with his knowledge and talents. He would be introducing the new and highly-effective convergent ex-maze procedure to a whole new sector of the country. It was exciting! I was just thankful that he had arrived in my area when he did and that he stayed here for the three years that I needed him. So for no other reason than to just say goodbye, he scheduled me for another visit at the end of the following month, about one week before his departure.

I left the office that day heavyhearted. It was definitely a time of mixed emotions for me. I do not get along with a lot of the people that I meet, and I am rarely comfortable with any doctors. Most doctors that I have had any experience with are elitist and condescending, taking offense at the first sign that you might be questioning their unilateral choice of treatment or their irreproachable orders. And heaven forbid, you should take a minute more of their time than you are being billed for or ask for technical information that is deemed only for doctors to know. My EP was a genuine, down-to-earth guy who, once he knew of my scientific background and inquisitive nature, freely shared as much (if not more) details as I could process – everything from the basics (and more) of the heart and circulatory system, my condition in general and specifics, the available medications and their methods of action, to all the other types of treatments and the risks of each as well as the risks of not treating it at all. That trust he placed in me drove me on to do even more research than I might have otherwise, which led me to have even more questions for him. But he liked to entertain questions and allowed me – nay, encouraged me – to be an equal partner in all the decisions that had to be made regarding my care and treatment. Yes, I have had other decent doctors that have treated me well and have respected my opinions, but I doubt that I will ever find another doctor like my first EP. That right there is incentive enough for me to try to stay healthy!

Life Goes On

Right before my July 2012 appointment with my EP, I had another short bout of a-fib, and curiously, it also struck almost six weeks after the previous bout – is this going to be the new pattern for me? Right around this time, I received yet another order for a battery of amiodaroine-related blood tests that I no longer needed. I promptly called my cardiology office and told them that my EP had taken me off the amio three months earlier, and I asked them to please stop sending me these orders for blood tests. They put me on hold, checked my file, and then came back and said that they found no record of my amio ever being stopped. They even went so far as to scold me, saying that I should <u>never</u> stop taking *any* prescribed medication without a doctor instructing me to do so. Great... but my doctor *did* order me to stop taking it! And just like the last time I called, they were very condescending and indignant with me. So I *may* have mouthed off a bit and made a derogatory remark or two... before frustration got the best of me, and I hung up.

Naturally, I mentioned this less-than-respectful treatment that I had received from his office staff when I saw my EP just a few days later. He didn't seem to care too much, though... after all, he was outta there! I also told him about the one lone bout of a-fib that I had had since I last saw him, and again, he found it unremarkable – I was still well within that one year post-op healing period. We spent the majority of this last appointment talking about the new EP lab at my hospital, which he had helped to design. He had promised to give me a tour of it once it was finished, but now he was leaving one month before it was even slated to open. He was not at all happy that he never got a chance to use it – in fact, he hadn't even seen it yet. But he did say that he'd leave word with my new EP (one of his colleagues who came up from Penn with him) to give me a tour once it opened. We exhausted our alloted 45 minutes, said our goodbyes and well wishes, and I left with a follow-up with the new guy tentatively scheduled for September.

About six weeks later, now like clockwork, another short bout of a-fib came and went, and before I knew it, so had the entire month of September... no confirmation call or mailed reminder for my cardiology appointment like I was used to getting. So I stopped the warfarin anyway at the end of the month per my previous EP's off-the-record opinion and also returned my home INR testing meter. I was so happy not to have to stab my fingers every week anymore. Then another month went by with still no word from my cardiology office, and I decided to call them to see what was up on their end.

They told me that their whole office was almost six months behind schedule since my old EP left, and that the new EP wouldn't be able to see me until at least February. They said they'd get back to me. I wasn't holding my breath.

In November, as what now seemed like it must surely have been a practical joke, yet *another* order for amiodarone tests arrived in the mail. Well, ha ha... the joke would be on them. I shredded it! I did not call the office, I did not receive a scolding, I did not pass "Go", and more importantly, I never received any more of these orders. I guess someone over there finally got the message, or maybe they just gave up. And in keeping with the "practical joke" theme, I got yet another short bout of a-fib right around that same time. It had been another six weeks... so of course it was "a-fib time". But this was the actual one-year point... so shouldn't I be healed by now? I just hoped these bouts would not go on for much longer. Yes, they were pretty short, and they only came every six weeks – even if that's as good as it were to get, it would be a huge success over what I had been living with before. Still, I wanted them to stop altogether so I could eventually forget about them and truly get back to normal 100%. How could I help this along? The only way an engineer knows... I would log my bouts and look for a trend!

When February rolled around, I received a letter of confirmation from my cardiology office for my follow-up appointment with my new EP – and it was in just a few days! Confirmation? This was the first that I had heard of it. I'm glad I went to my mailbox that day. I was looking forward to officially meeting this new EP (actually, we had already met, briefly - he is the one who discharged me after I was admitted for that bout of left atrial flutter in February 2011). At this point, I had had no a-fib at all in three full months since that last minor episode, so I was feeling pretty good – both physically and mentally. But then I went in to see my new EP. Like a recurring bad dream, he broached the subject of me stopping my amiodarone without a doctor's order. Are you kidding me??? My doctor told me to stop it way back in June! I just about flipped! I asked him to please contact my old EP (I had his new email address if this guy needed it!) and verify that he did tell me to stop taking it. He really did want me to stop it – I am not making this up. I guess he just never recorded it in my file. It was his last few days there - he was probably preoccupied with his impending departure and relocation. Ugh, what a huge amount of stress such a small oversight had caused me.

Then this new EP asked me about my warfarin... I knew that he knew that I had stopped taking it because it was in my file that I had returned my home testing meter, and I am sure that his all-seeing eye had also spotted that I had stopped refilling my prescription. I told him that my old EP said that, if it were up to him, he would have stopped the warfarin in September (because I'd have been off the amiodarone for five months at that time) – given, of course, that the chronic a-fib had not returned by then. This new guy flat out told me that he disagreed with that decision, and I guess when he saw that I wasn't buying it, he actually went so far as to say that my old EP had left a note for him (my new EP) in my file saying that he (my old EP) felt that I should remain on warfarin for the rest of my life. And I flat out didn't believe this because it was completely opposite of what my old EP had told me at my last visit right before he left. So I asked to see this "note". Of course, I didn't expect him to show me anything or to even have anything to show. And he did not let me down. I *really* don't appreciate being lied to.

Things had started off pretty rocky with this new guy and were not getting any better as our visit progressed. He certainly wasn't the kind of doctor that my first EP was. He wasn't even the same kind of person. My old EP thought I would get along with him well because this guy was an engineer like I was before he became a doctor. Yeah, well, he certainly <u>did</u> have the personality of an engineer, which just does not jive with me. When I told this guy that I was already off the warfarin for five months and that I wasn't about to go back on it, he told me that the only way that he would "allow" me to be off warfarin was if I agreed to more surgery to implant a loop recorder in my chest for the next *three years* to prove to him that I no longer had any a-fib.

This was an obvious "cover your butt" move on his part. He did not know me at all and had zero familiarity with my case. So he did not trust that I could feel it every single time when I was in a-fib. I do understand the "better safe than sorry" mindset, but my old EP knew that I could tell whenever I was in a-fib and knew that I wasn't foolish enough to take the risk of refusing warfarin if I thought that I really needed it.

Couldn't he have told this to my new doctor in this supposed "note" of his? So even though I completely understood where this new guy was coming from, I would not be strong-armed. Seeing as how it was, at that time, already more than 13 months since my severe chronic a-fib had subsided and an entire three months since I had had any a-fib at all, I felt very comfortable refusing to go back on warfarin. We agreed to disagree and just left it at that.

The last issue that we discussed before I was able to get out of there was my blood pressure... high again. The doctor told me that the behavior of my blood pressure over time (my lifelong history of borderline high blood pressure gradually increasing and then continuing to increase even as more drugs were added) is indicative of a genetic condition called "essential hypertension", whereby the body's system of regulating blood pressure gets confused and thinks it needs to be higher than it should be. It is not uncommon for sufferers of essential hypertension to be maxed out on one drug and then have additional drugs added to their regimin... some people end up on five or six medications just for their blood pressure. I was already on max doses of lisinopril and metoprolol, and now this doctor wanted to add 25mg qd of spironolactone (Aldactone®). This is the same drug used (in larger quantities) for chemical castration of sex offenders and for feminizing male-to-female sex-changers. Even at the low dosage he wanted me on, gynecomastia (development of female breasts), hypogonadism (shrinking of the testicles), and sexual dysfunction are possible side effects. Fortunately, after taking this drug for 18 months now, I have experienced none of these. And my blood pressure is stable, too, so the dosage won't have to be upped any time soon (I hope). I left the office with another follow up scheduled for September.

Over the ensuing six months, I had experienced only one single, very short bout (minutes) of a-fib. I felt very good about that, but as my recent experiences were teaching me, every time I began to feel good about something, my cardiology office's staff would find a way to throw a monkey wrench into it. This time, when a few of my prescriptions had expired, I called in to the office to have them renewed. Standard practice. Several of these were renewed without incident, but on two other occasions I was scolded and told in a very demeaning way that I shouldn't keep bothering them with this and that my family doctor should be regulating and handling the renewal of all my prescription medications. I am not accustomed to being routinely treated like crap, especially by supposed professionals, and these two incidents now made a total of five times that the people of this practice – who I was paying to help me, no less – disrespected and talked down to me. Last straw? Yep. I had had about all that I felt comfortable taking from them, and I decided, then and there, that it was time to start seeing my family doctor again (after almost ten years!). I'd rather give him my money, anyway, and let him handle my prescriptions (just as my cardiology office suggested). So no more a-fib... why did I need to see the EP anymore, right? Exactly. I cancelled my September appointment. Arrivederci!

In November, I received a notice from my insurance carrier that my current policy had to be cancelled at the end of the year due to regulations imposed by the Affordable Care Act. Money was already tight for me, so I dropped the policy right away, a month early. Without insurance, now I really could not afford a visit with an EP (as the specialist of specialists, they rake in top-dollar). So when his office kept hounding me to make a new appointment, I told them that I was cancelling until further notice. That was nine months ago at the time of writing. Since recovering from the ex-maze procedure, I have now been in NSR for 31 months with only a handful of insignificant bouts of a-fib during that time. Six bouts were in 2012 (all within the one-year post-surgical healing period), then only two bouts in all of 2013, and only two bouts so far this year.

My family doctor is now gladly managing my prescription medications. Don't get me wrong... I was happy to have a great EP nearby when I needed one, but I just don't see the point in seeing an unpleasant doctor in a chaotic and unfriendly environment on a regular, ongoing basis now that there is nothing for him to treat or even follow up on. If for some reason I ever do need an EP again, I will probably seek one out at one of the other cardiology practices in my area. It is a real shame that my original practice (which truly was my practice of choice in the beginning, and for good reason) has just gone so downhill so fast and has literally fallen apart on all levels after my first EP left them. I fear that it may be quite a while before they recover... if at all.

Since I have had the ex-maze surgery, I have also noticed a marked difference in my PVCs, which I've been experiencing now for the past 40 years. Prior to the surgery, my PVCs came on a fairly regular basis and usually in response to physical exertion, stress, overeating (or just eating), or GI pressure or movement. They would occur almost daily in the presence of these various "triggers" but then cease when the associated trigger went away or was removed. This behavior persisted pretty much throughout my life and remained about the same even after I was put on medications for my atrial fibrillation. It was only after my heart calmed down following the convergent ex-maze surgery that I noticed that my PVCs began coming more in the form of "storms".

That is to say that, post-ex-maze, the same triggers seem to initiate the onset of PVCs, but now when the stimulus is removed, the PVCs will continue to come for days on end... for as long as about 15 days, so far. This behavior is very similar to a typical bout of a-fib that I might have had before the surgery, but now without the a-fib. Curious. My first EP told me that, even though they are unrelated and occur in two completely separate parts of the heart, there was a little-understood connection between PVCs and atrial fibrillation. It is also interesting to note that lying on my left side, which often used to trigger my bouts of a-fib (but never PVCs), can now sometimes also initiate these PVC storms. I guess this will be something else for me to study.

In addition to this new "storm" behavior, I now seem to be completely immune to PVCs during the periods in between these storms. When "PVC time" is over, there is now a five-to six-week long "refractory period" of sorts, during which nothing that I do will trigger a single PVC. Considering how easily and consistently I got PVCs before the surgery, I am almost more amazed by this unexpected side effect of the surgery than the success it has shown in treating my a-fib (after all, that's what it was designed to do). I think that if I were an EP, I would be *studying* these mysterious PVCs rather than just telling my patients to ignore them. I'm not quite sure just what I would be looking for, but I can't help thinking that there must be something important to be learned from them. Time will tell!

I have also noticed a few other things in the more than two and a half years since the surgery. Most noticeable is the lump in my throat, which I had assumed was my thyroid – either a swelling of this gland or a tumor on it. I first noticed it in January 2012, at which point I had been taking amiodarone for nine months. My mind goes right to the link between the two because amiodarone is very high in iodine and is well known to cause thyroid problems. By the way, only after stopping the amiodarone did I learn that this drug is stored in the body's fat cells and has an *exceptionally* long half-life – an average of about two months but possibly as long as five months! Generally, a drug is considered to be "cleared" from your system after ten half-lives (when its level is is $1/2^{10}$ or about 0.1%), but realistically, most drugs fall below a significant level long before that... let's just say five half-lives (or at about 3%). For amiodarone, this comes to a whopping 10 to 25 months for it to drop to 3% of it's original concentration in your system. And to add insult to injury amio's primary metabolite (what your body breaks the drug down into), desethyl-amiodarone, also has a very long half-life and also has toxic effects similar to its parent, amiodarone. This metabolite could hang around yet another year or more after the amio is completely metabolized. Finally, there are the NANDAI compounds (non-amiodarone, non-desethyamiodarone iodine compounds) that remain in the body even longer still. Altogether, the amiodarone can, literally, leave its mark on the user for from three to as many as eight years (using the ten half-life rule) after he/she stops taking it and continue to wreak its havoc during that time. A compelling reason to try to avoid it from the start.

Anyway... back to my thyroid. Some other things that pointed me toward suspecting that I had a thyroid problem were the constant insomnia and low energy levels and the trouble losing weight that I had been and continue to experience. Particularly that I had lost most of the remainder of the weight that I had gained during the first two years that I had suffered from a-fib shortly after the ex-maze surgery, but even though I was still on the very same low-carb diet that I have been on since late-2008 and my activity level has since increased, my weight loss had plateaued about five to ten pounds short of my goal and has been stalled there for over a year. It has only recently began picking up (however slowly) since the spring and summer weather has arrived.

In March of this year, when I finally decided to see my family doctor after a ten year hiatus, I told him about my suspected thyroid issues and that I thought that they might be a result of the twelve months of amiodarone that I took two years earlier. He told me that he has never seen amiodarone cause thyroid problems, and looking way back in my file to 2003, he thought that the other symptoms that I described were probably just coincidental and that the lump in my throat might be a swollen esophagus from the same GERD that I had been diagnosed with back then. I reminded him that he had put me on omeprazole for the GERD and that I had been taking it daily ever since and that, because of that, I no longer suffered from heartburn. But he went on to explain that a person will still have GERD even without feeling heartburn, and it can still cause irritation of the esophagus. He felt it would be best for me to see a GE and have it looked into... maybe even have another EGD.

Regardless of this new information, I remained convinced that my symptoms were thyroid-related. In a last-ditch effort to convince my doctor of even a remote possibility that my theory was valid, I told him about the three nuclear medicine studies that I had done as well as five head and chest CTs, countless chest x-rays, and the 14 total hours of heart procedures, both using a fluoroscope. The look on his face changed with every word that I uttered until he seemed pensive and concerned. I got his attention! He agreed to send me for a thyroid ultrasound (he chose the ultrasound rather than the old-time "upper GI", the one with the barium sulfate milk shake, to spare me any additional radiation exposure). So I went for the ultrasound, and the results came back – my thyroid is mildly heterogeneous (slightly larger on one side) but otherwise unremarkable, as are my parathyroid and parotid glands. That means that I will need to see a GE after all to have my esophagus checked. Mmm... barium. And more radiation. Does it come as a surprise that I haven't scheduled this test yet? Soon (said the procrastinator).

My family doctor also sent me for a blood test to check my thyroid, lipids, and liver enzymes. My thyroid (TSH *and* free T4) tested normal, lipids were high though (total cholesterol over 240 and LDL of 170) so he wanted to try switching drugs – the pravastatin that I was on clearly wasn't doing its job anymore. He told me that doubling the dosage of statins only lowers cholesterol by a mere 6%. So to get my cholesterol down to the range that he wanted it to be in (total below 170, LDL below 70), my dosage would have had to have been doubled <u>six</u> times – a whopping 64 times the dose that I was already taking. That would be 1,280mg per day! Probably lethal, at least to my liver. He thought that atorvastatin (Lipitor®) might work a little better since it acts via a different metabolic pathway. Another blood test three months later would bear this out – total cholesterol 160 and LDL 100. Good, but not great. He doubled my atorvastatin... we'll test it again in November.

Another issue that I have had, which also started around the same time as the suspected thyroid problems, was what seems to me like low blood sugar. Or at least unstable blood sugar. I am often shaky and dizzy first thing in the morning if I do not eat something almost immediately. And whenever I go too long between meals, the same thing happens. Eating something with carbohydrates (sugar or starch) resolves the symptoms in about 15 minutes, so I am fairly certain that it has something to do with my blood sugar. I have been managing it myself for the last two plus years, but once the mysterious lump in my throat is figured out, I will bring it to my doctor's attention. Beta blockers are known to raise fasting blood sugar levels and may also cause insulin resistance (which is, in essence, type II diabetes). And since I have been on a high dose of metoprolol for quite a while now, this is a concern. Or it could be another artifact of the amiodarone... or even of the radiation. Or it might not be any of these. My fasting blood sugar was measured several times at around the mid-80s, which is about normal. So it's just another mystery to be solved. More tests, more money.

That does it for the issues that have had the most negative impact on my life since getting rid of my a-fib and flutter, but there are others of less significance, too. For example, even though my AST and ALT (liver enzymes) have been steadily declining back into the mid-normal range, my bilirubin has been slowly creeping up – now 1.9 and rising. So... liver problem or no liver problem? It isn't affecting how I feel, but it is curious, and I would like to know the reason for it. My doctor told me that many things (diet, meds, etc.) can make the level go up, and that it doesn't mean anything unless it continues to go up or suddenly jumps very high.

Also under the "strange" category... since that second time that I was on amiodarone, I have been experiencing localized pilomotor reflex action – in other words, spontaneous goosebumps only on small isolated spots on my body and not in response to any change in temperature. This reflex is mediated by the autonomic nervous system, so it may be some sort of neurological problem. Similarly, I have also been experiencing localized hyperhidrosis (aka "excessive sweating"), but just on my wrists. Again, this is not in response to temperature change... it just happens. Both of these problems are so weird and so seemingly unimportant that I have not told my doctor about them yet. They might mean something when looked at together with everything else, though, so I have not been ignoring them completely.

I also still have what I suspect to be Raynaud's syndrome or at least something with similar symptoms. I think it might be from the drugs that I am or was on, but my family doctor thinks it is just Raynaud's syndrome. He also thinks that it is mere coincidence that it only started after I began taking metoprolol (interesting how five other doctors agree that metoprolol was the likely cause). So without a referral from my doctor for this problem, I have no idea who to see about it or if it is even worth investigating. And there is the slight decrease in fine motor skills that may also be related to nerve damage caused by these same medications or could be due to the micro-infarcts that I mentioned in the beginning of the book. Totally unrelated are renal insufficiency that I think I might have and some odd visual disturbances since being on amiodarone (both known issues). These problems can wait, however, until I have all the other issues figured out and under control. My two most recent blood tests, by the way, indicated a GFR (glomerular filtration rate) of 107 and 83, respectively, which my doctor tells me are very good numbers, and they mean that my kidneys are functioning well. So mysteries still abound!

Last, my blood pressure was, recently, checked at my family doctor's office and read in the mid-160s over low-100s. High! He checked it several times during that visit, and it was roughly the same each time. I told him that my blood pressure has actually been so low that I sometimes feel as though I might pass out when I stand up. He held off on adjusting my meds but wanted me to check and log my blood pressure at home for two weeks and bring him a report at my next visit. Can do! The at-rest blood pressures that I measured at home – three times a day for two weeks – were all in the 90s to 120s over the 60s to 80s. So I guess it really is just "white coat syndrome", though I never feel the least bit anxious when visiting him (he doesn't even wear a white coat!). At my next visit two weeks later, I must have been more relaxed – 130ish over 80ish. Given that and the readings that I had logged at home, he did not adjust my medications.

Besides these few relatively minor health issues (and the fact that I still cannot tolerate alcohol and am buried under a huge amount of debt from my medical bills), things have been going great since undergoing the convergent ex-maze. It truly has eradicated my chronic a-fib. Some of my energy has returned due in part, I believe, to being in NSR but also due in part to losing most of the a-fib weight. Since I am still on the beta blocker and continue to suffer its side effects, and because I am still not sleeping well, I do not yet feel quite as good as I did before my a-fib started in 2006. But I also have to accept that that may never happen. All things considered, I feel much better now than I have in a long time. I have been able to get my businesses back on track. I have been able to do some remodeling around my home (which translates to "I have been able to start even more perpetually-unfinished projects."). And I have been able to get back to spending more time with my friends and family.

Just one month after returning home from the ex-maze, I began working on a tongue-in-cheek photo book of local public restrooms, which I published about a year later. I also jumped back into the music scene, co-producing, recording, mixing, and publishing a second album for my friends' band. Perhaps most significantly, though, I became aware of and joined several a-fib, SVT, and cardiac arrhythmia-related forums on Facebook. I found them all to be great resources for people who were looking for support in dealing with these conditions, but the information and education aspect seemed to be sorely lacking in the existing groups. I do understand some people's need for emotional support when dealing with something as scary and depressing as a chronic heart arrhythmia, and the groups that I found did a great job of filling this need. But I felt there was still a glaring need for a group focused on the education aspect and the sharing of solid information relevant to atrial fibrillation and supra-ventricular tachycardias, so I created a new group to fill this void. I set it up as "closed", which keeps members' posts private and accessible only to other members (as opposed to some of the other groups that are set as "public" and allow anyone on the Internet to view their contents. I felt that that was patently inappropriate for and not conducive to the sharing of personal medical information).

It wasn't long after I created the group that new members started pouring in. And now at over 2,300 members worldwide, the **Atrial Fibrillation Information Exchange** is the fastest growing and most complete resource for a-fib and other heart arrhythmia information on Facebook. It has drawn the attention of several national health organizations and healthcare professionals from around the world and has afforded me the opportunity to become involved in national focus groups and discussion panels and to voice my opinions and concerns directly to various manufacturers and other professionals in the healthcare industry. This group has truly allowed me to turn the lemons of a-fib that life had dumped on me into the copious amounts of lemonade that now quench my thirst for recompense. And it is at the behest and encouragement of the more active members of my group that I have written this book with the hope that it may provide some comfort to those who feel like they are struggling with this soul-sucking condition alone.

In addition to spawning this book, the various discussions in my group and the numerous questions posed to me by its members on a daily basis have made me aware of another void within our community – software that can actually analyze the heart arrhythmias that patients and sufferers are likely already tracking in some way on their own. My epiphany was that, if the subtle relationships that may exist between patterns in the patient's arrhythmias and other patterns in his/her lifestyle or in the natural cycles within his/her own body can be identified and quantified, then the sufferer can be alerted to these and may be empowered to effect some level of change on his/her own and maybe even realize an improved quality of life because of it, all the while minimizing the need for potentially harmful medications.

So I have begun development of an application that will do just that. It is still in its infancy (a mere embryo) and will not be ready for beta testing until some time in 2105, but I am confident that it will prove successful at putting some control back into the hands of at least some patients. To be clear, this software is in no way intended as a cure for heart arrhythmias or as a replacement for real medical treatment. It is just one more tool in the toolbox that the arrhythmia sufferer already has at his/her disposal. Used prudently and in the right combination, these tools may help some of us to slow down the progression of their arrhythmias or reduce their reliance on medications for the level of relief that they seek. And as all of us arrhythmia sufferers know, any help is better than none at all. It is my sincere hope that this software will help at least some of the heart arrhythmia sufferers out there to cope with their conditions just a little bit better.

PROGNOSIS

This is the last chapter, so I will give you guys a break... it will not be about me. Well, not *specifically* about me. It will pertain to everyone who suffers from, or who has suffered from, atrial fibrillation. That's me <u>and</u> you. All of us. So... what do you think *our* prognosis is? I'll tell you, the prognosis for each and every one of us is a big, fat...

Now why would I say something like that? That's not very encouraging. Unfortunately, with so little known about what causes many, if not most, of the nearly 400,000 new cases of chronic lone atrial fibrillation that are diagnosed every year, it is difficult to take measures to prevent its return once you think that you might have been successfully "cured" (though there really is no cure, per se, for a-fib – the best we can hope for right now is to find a way to block the signals that cause it). In fact, the mere reality that you have developed a-fib could mean that you had already had some sort of genetic propensity to do so. It may be something hereditary, or it could just be a congenital abnormality that makes you more susceptible, just waiting for the right condition or set of conditions that create the "perfect storm" that allows the arrhythmia to take hold. Does this mean that these people will never be free of a-fib? I don't think it means that, but it does mean that these people will have to be forever vigilant to avoid those conditions that could possibly precipitate the return of their a-fib or other any arrhythmias.

So what might these conditions be? It is already known that hypertension and pulmonary hypertension can cause enlargement of the entire heart or left atrium and ultimately lead to the onset of chronic a-fib. Other heart conditions are also known to sometimes lead to a-fib. So keeping your blood pressure under control, and treating any sleep apnea (which can cause pulmonary hypertension) or heart conditions that you may have would probably be good advice. Dehydration, electrolyte imbalances, and stimulants, as well as alcohol and other drugs can also cause acute bouts of a-fib, and then if these bouts occur too frequently or last too long, the heart can begin to remodel, making the a-fib more likely to become chronic. So avoiding those things that can bring on acute bouts might also be advisable in the long run. And if you do all of this, you will prevent the a-fib from returning, right? Not necessarily. There may be many things beyond our control and even beyond our current understanding that can lead to the development of a-fib, so try as we might, it could always return without notice in spite of all our efforts. And this is especially true for those who are already predisposed to it in some way.

But my doctor told me that my high blood pressure probably caused my a-fib, and now I take blood pressure medicine to keep it "normal", so if I have surgery now to get rid of my a-fib, then it won't come back... right? Again, not necessarily. There is absolutely no way to determine with any certainty what precisely caused your a-fib in the first place. If you have had untreated high blood pressure for a long time, then yes, it is likely that it contributed to the development of your chronic a-fib. But it is also likely that your and your doctor's investigation into any causes ended right there once that single possible contributing factor was identified. Suppose your a-fib was caused by both high blood pressure **and** some other less obvious factor or factors. You stopped looking after finding "high blood pressure", and now you will never find the other one or ones... you are lulled into a false sense of security thinking that all you need to do is to treat that one condition. You DO need to treat your high blood pressure, that's for sure, but that does not mean that there aren't any additional factors at play, as well, and that your a-fib will now magically never return. OK? Make sense? I think you get it... I won't belabor the point.

So what hope is there then, really? Well, every day I tell myself to do whatever it takes to make it just one more day. Sound stupid? Here's my reasoning. You never know what tomorrow will bring! Suppose there is a treatment available to you now that you are a candidate for, but your doctor tells you that it may only provide temporary relief – that it is <u>not</u> a long-term solution. If it is your best option at the time, why not go for it... who knows what treatment options will then be available in a few months or a year or whenever you need it again? Technology is advancing so rapidly in this epoch that better and better treatments for a-fib are being thought of and developed all the time. This is especially true right now as the number of cases of a-fib diagnosed annually has skyrocketed in recent years. The market is ripe, and it has been attracting lots of attention from the drug companies, medical device manufacturers, researchers, and up and coming doctors alike. And the recently-formed National Association of Integrated A-fib Centers (NAIAC) – a coalition of doctors, facilities, and other providers who employ an integrated approach to treatment of a-fib and other cardiac arrhythmias – is spearheading the effort to share practical data, research results, and resources in order to improve education across the industry of the best and most current treatment practices available.

It was not that long ago, for example, that there was no PVI ablation procedure available. And then one day, there was!

And the face of a-fib treatment was changed forever with this much more successful procedure. Likewise, there were no mini-maze procedures until one day, there was! And the face of a-fib treatment was changed, again. The same can be said for some of the drugs used to treat a-fib. For example, researchers are finding ways to lower the dosages of some of the more dangerous but still highly effective antiarrhythmic drugs by combining them with other safer drugs to get the same if not better a-fib stopping performance out of them. And once effective reversal agents are widely available for the NOAs, they will likely gain the acceptance that their manufacturers have long been hoping for and offer a more convenient protection from a-fib stroke than warfarin.

They may not seem like a major advancement, but these new oral anticoagulants have the potential to change the lives of a-fib sufferers. Not only are they much more convenient to use than warfarin with no required testing and dosage adjustments (as of yet!) and no known dietary restrictions, but they can also be taken only as needed because they reach therapeutic levels in the blood stream within only a few hours rather than the 3-5 days that it takes warfarin to have the same effect. The latter benefit, of course, depends upon each individual doctor's trust in his/her patient's ability to identify when he/she goes into a-fib and to know when he/she should take the drug. I foresee the day, however, when (enter technology) an implantable monitor with a built-in alarm option will tell the patient when he/she is in a-fib and when to take his/her anticoagulant, alleviating the worries of the patient as well as the concerns of his/her doctor. In time and with enough money, the possibilities truly are endless.

Or rather than sensing the a-fib and merely sounding a warning, why not take action and stop it? Right now, implantable defibrillators are only used for ventricular fibrillation because direct electrical defibrillation of the heart (cardioversion) is painful. During v-fib, the patient is usually unconscious and will not feel it, so shock away! Shocking a lucid a-fib patient would be very uncomfortable, though, especially if it happened over and over (as many of us go in and out of a-fib multiple times throughout the day). Enter technology... how about a shockless cardioversion? Researchers have found a way to genetically implant light-activated ion channels into the heart muscle, allowing a "light defibrillator" to be implanted in the patient. By turning on an array of lights when fibrillation is detected (this would work on both atrial and ventricular fibrillation), the heart would be painlessly returned to normal sinus rhythm. This technique could provide a welcome option for certain cases of both a-fib and v-fib.

Along these same lines of innovation is the FIRM (Focal Impulse and Rotor Modulation) ablation. This is a "hotspot" type of ablation similar to those used to treat certain types of SVT. It involves the identification and elimination of the individual points on the myocardium that are responsible for the patient's a-fib. This is a very new procedure but seems to hold promise for treating a particular classification of a-fib.

And even further down the road, I believe we may be seeing these now minimally-invasive procedures (ablations, mini-mazes, etc.) being performed completely non-invasively through the magic of stereotactic radio-surgery. Procedures of this type are performed using multiple low-dose beams of radiation administered at various different angles through the external tissue and focused on the point that is to be destroyed (or "ablated"). At this focal point, the dosages of the individual beams add up to a lethal dose, but only at this point, deep inside the body... the surrounding area remains relatively unscathed. These procedures are currently used to treat otherwise inoperable cancerous tumors, but there has also been exciting recent development in the arena of stereotactic radiosurgical cardiac ablationss. Hang on one more day, and you might be first to get a Star Trek-style PVI!

In the less distant future, and even in the present, there have been improvements to existing technology that promise to increase the success rates of some of the conventional procedures. Advancements such as the Smart Touch® RF ablation catheter... it has a pressure-sensitive tip and provides better positioning feedback to the doctor performing the ablation, allowing him to make more accurate lesions while reducing the level of risk associated with the stray energy that is emitted throughout this procedure. Likewise, several flexible-tipped and vacuum-positioned ablation catheter designs are also being tested with the intent to improve the accuracy of the lesions formed during the PVI and convergent ex-maze procedures.

There are other advancements that we are seeing today that may also help improve the quality of life for some a-fib sufferers. New DNA tests to identify those with hereditary factors for developing arrhythmias can lead to preventive therapies, allowing the arrhythmias to be better controlled or maybe even avoided, altogether. The MediGuide® catheter tracking system aims at reducing the amount of radiation the patient receives during an ablation by tracking the catheter using a magnetic GPS-like system, greatly reducing the need for a fluoroscope to position the catheter. Devices such as the Atricure® clip and the Watchman® filter and procedures such as the Lariat® aim to eliminate the risk of clots either breaking free and entering circulation during or after long bouts of uncontrolled a-fib or even forming in th4e first place, thus eliminating the stroke risk without the need for anticoagulants and their side effects (both the potentially dangerous and the not-so-dangerous). New devices, such as the Remedē® implantable diaphragm "pacemaker", may be useful in treating certain types of sleep apnea – this is not directly related to a-fib, but since many of us a-fib sufferers also suffer from, and must be treated for, sleep apnea, this device could provide some with a preferred alternative to the time-tested treatment of a CPAP (continuous positive airway pressure) mask, which many find difficult, if not impossible, to sleep with (and the only current alternative to a UPPP).

Besides the new devices, meds, and procedures that are coming down the pike, there have also been recent reports on a number of interesting research studies. One in particular that caught my attention is the DECAAF study, which found that fibrotic tissue (scar tissue, to you and me) in the wall of the left atrium may be the primary cause of certain types of chronic atrial fibrillation, and that the ablation of this tissue, alone, may offer better outcomes than the PVI ablation. This is because, as this study found, a PVI will typically ablate *some* of the fibrotic tissue that exists in the left atrium, but not all of it, but that that tissue is only ablated purely by chance, not by design. What exactly all of this means to the future of atrial fibrillation ablation remains to be seen. To be sure, many more studies and much more research will have to be done to determine how these findings may best be put into practice, but studies like this are divining new answers every day... many to questions that we didn't even know to ask!

Another study, the ADVICE study, has shown that there may be electrically dormant portions of the pulmonary veins that can become active after an ablation, causing the arrhythmia to return. That's good to know! The study also found that, through the use of adenosine during the ablation procedure, these dormant areas can be more easily identified and then addressed. Trials of this method have shown a **50% reduction** in the incidence of return of the arrhythmia following the ablation. That's huge! And this is not a particularly high-tech advancement, just a new way to use the drugs and procedures that the medical community already has at its disposal and is already comfortable using. So no additional learning curve or risks. With more research dollars pouring into the field of atrial fibrillation and heart arrhythmias in general, I believe we could see many more innovations in treatment such as this in coming years.

I leave it up to (and encourage!) you, the reader, to research the things that I have mentioned in this chapter – and throughout this book, for that matter – on your own and to draw your own conclusions. I also advise that everyone stay current on all the relevant news... there is much more worthy of note than I have mentioned here. With these few specific examples, though, I hope that I was able to offer ample support for my recommendation to do whatever it takes today to make it to tomorrow... it should now be obvious that there are plenty of reasons to do so. And while I still stand firmly by my prognosis for the a-fib suffer being the big "?", I do want to emphatically footnote that with the most positive attitude towards what I believe the future holds for us all. Stay vigilant, stay strong, and stay educated! Not only is knowledge the best treatment for a-fib, it is our strongest ally in the battle against the anxiety that can accompany it. And finally, if your doctor will not listen to you, educate you, answer your questions, and address your concerns, find one who will!

Prognosis

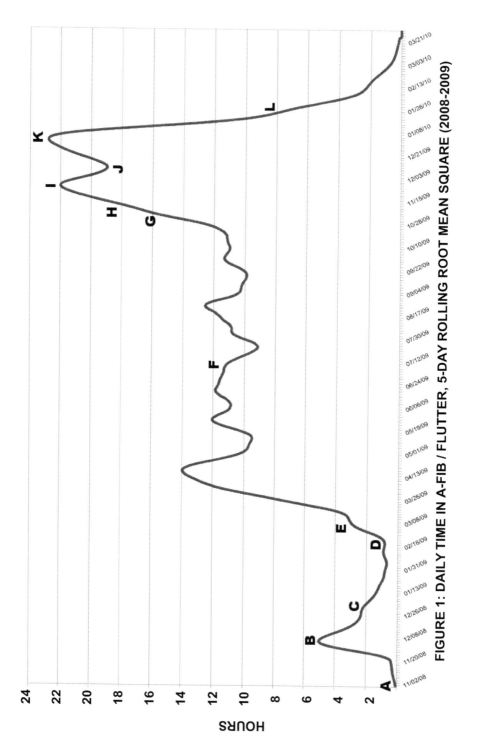

FIGURE 1: DAILY TIME IN A-FIB / FLUTTER, 5-DAY ROLLING ROOT MEAN SQUARE (2008-2009)

Appendix

<u>LEGEND</u>

A – Started logging one week after starting metoprolol succinate, 25mg qd.

B – Metoprolol succinate increased to 50mg qd.

C – Metoprolol succinate increased to 100mg qd.

D – First bout of atrial flutter experienced.

E – Started digoxin, 0.25mg qd.

F – Digoxin stopped. Switched to metoprolol tartrate, increased to 100mg bid.

G – Started flecainide, 300mg tid.

H – Flecainide stopped. Start propafenone, 450mg tid.

I – Scheduled cardioversion date (cancelled). Stopped propafenone.

J – Atrial flutter returns. Propafenone restarted, 450mg tid.

K – Cardioversion performed. Propafenone stopped. Started amiodarone, 400mg qd.

L – RF catheter ablation (Pulmonary Vein Isolation) performed.

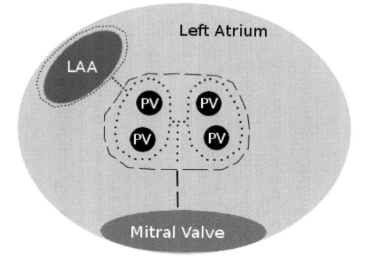

FIGURE 2a: PVI Ablation lesions (interior view)

PV – four Pulmonary Veins, LAA – opening of the Left Atrial Appendage

Pulmonary veins are isolated by enclosing lesions either in pairs (coarse dotted line) or all in one block (dashed line). In both cases, a lesion is generally also created between the pulmonary vein lesion(s) and the mitral valve. Some doctors also isolate the left atrial appendage (fine dotted line).

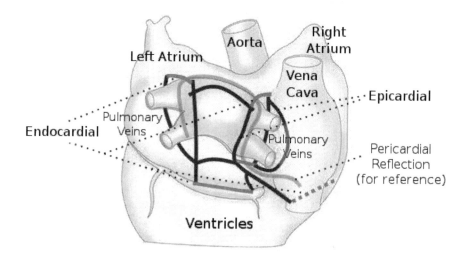

FIGURE 2b: Convergent Ex-maze lesions (posterior view)

Appendix

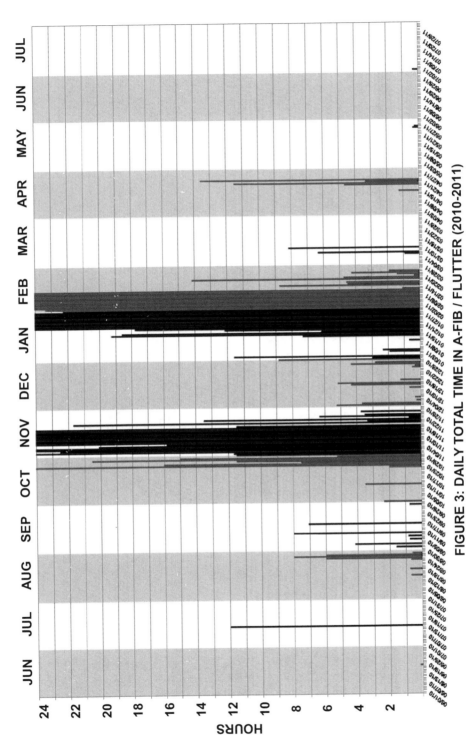

FIGURE 3: DAILY TOTAL TIME IN A-FIB / FLUTTER (2010-2011)

253

Appendix

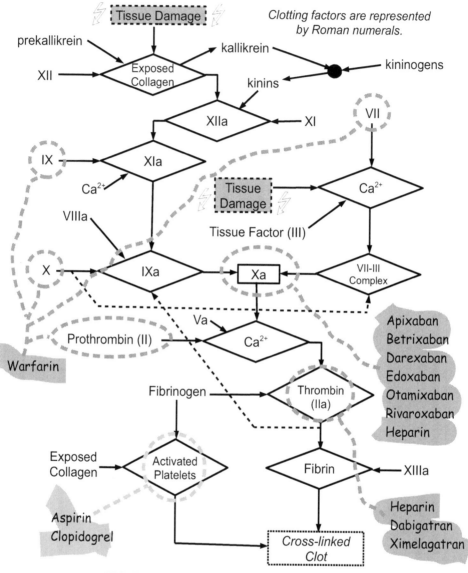

FIGURE 4: Clotting (Coagulation) Cascade

This simplified diagram of the chain of chemical reactions that are responsible for blood coagulation should illustrate that clotting is a far more complex process than a simple change in the blood's viscosity. Common anticoagulants shown in gray do not "thin" the blood but rather interrupt this chain of reactions. It is also easy to see on this graphic that clots can still form in the presence of aspirin (an antiplatelet, <u>not</u> an anticoagulant). Aspirin is **not** effective against a-fib stroke.

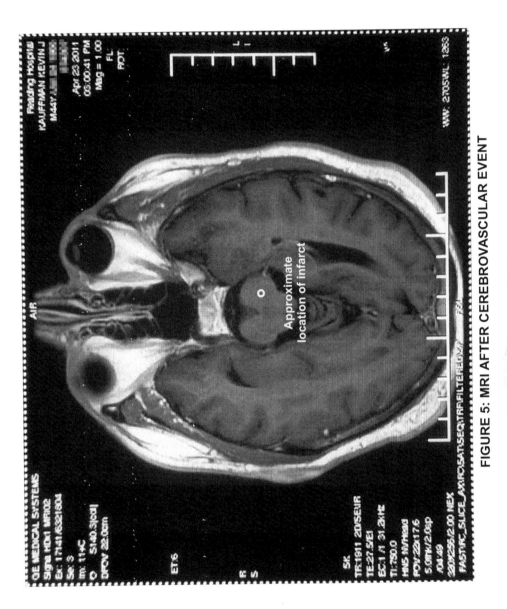

Approximate location of infarct

FIGURE 5: MRI AFTER CEREBROVASCULAR EVENT

Appendix

LIST OF ACRONYMS

This is a list of some of the heart-related acronyms that you may encounter in this book, medical journals and texts, online discussion forums, and in reports from your doctor or hospital.

AA: Antiarrhythmic
AAA: Antiarrhythmic Agent or
 Abdominal Aortic Aneurysm
AAD: Antiarrhythmic Drug
AB: Atrial Bigeminy
ABE: Acute Bacterial Endocarditis
ABG: Arterial Blood Gas
ABI: Ankle-Brachial Index
ACE: Angiotensin Converting Enzyme
ACLS: Advanced Cardiac Life Support
AE: Atrial Ectopy
AEB: Atrial Ectopic Beats
AED: Automated External Defibrillator
AEM: Ambulatory Electrocardiogram Monitoring
AF, Afib, or A-fib: Atrial Fibrillation
AFL or AFl: Atrial Flutter
AI: Aortic Insufficiency
AICD: Automated Implantable Cardioverter/Defibrillator
AIVR: Accelerated Idioventricular Rhythm
AMI: Acute Myocardial Infarction
AP: Apical Pulse
APB: Atrial Premature Beat
APC: Atrial Premature Complex
AR: Aortic Root
ARB: Angiotensin Receptor Blocker
ARVC: Arrhythmogenic Right Ventricular Cardiomyopathy
AS: Aortic Stenosis or
 Atrial Salvo
ASA: Atrial Septal Aneurysm or
 Acetylsalicylic Acid (a.k.a. aspirin)
ASD: Atrial Septal Defect
ASHD: Arteriosclerotic Heart Disease
ASO: Arteriosclerosis Obliterans
AT: Atrial Tachycardia

Appendix

ATP: Antitachycardia Pacing
ATR: Antitachycardia Response
AV: Atrioventricular (as in "AV node") or
    Aortic Valve
AVR: Accelerated Ventricular Rhythm
AVRT: Atrioventricular Reciprocating Tachycardia
AVNRT: Atriaoventricular Node Reentrant Tachycardia
BAV: Bicuspid Aortic Valve
BAVD: Bicuspid Aortic Valve Disease
BB: Beta Blocker
BBB: Bundle Branch Block
BID: twice a day
BP: Blood Pressure
BPM: Beats Per Minute
CA: Coronary Artery
CABG: Coronary Artery Bypass Graft
CAD: Coronary Artery Disease
CAG: Coronary Angiography or
    Coronary Artery Graft
CAGS: Coronary Artery Graft Surgery
CAT: Computed Axial Tomography
CCB: Calcium Channel Blocker
CCCU: Critical Coronary Care Unit
CCU: Coronary Care Unit
CCF: Congestive Coronary Failure (same as CHF)
CHADS2: stroke risk score comprised of one point each for
    CHF, Hypertension, Age>74, Diabetes mellitus, and 2
    points for prior Stroke
CH2ADS2-VASc: same as above but 2 points for Hypertension
    and adding one point each for Vascular disease, Age>64,
and Sex category (female)
CHD: Coronary Heart Disease or
    Congenital Heart Disease
CHF: Congestive Heart Failure (same as CCF)
CICU: Coronary Intensive Care Unit
CK: Creatinine Phosphokinase
CM: Cardiomyopathy
CO: Cardiac Output or
    carbon monoxide

Appendix

CO2: carbon dioxide
COPD: Chronic Obstructive Pulmonary Disease
COU: Coronary Observation Unit
CP: Chest Pain
CPAP: Continuous Positive Airway Pressure
CPK: Creatinine Phosphokinase
CPR: Cardiopulmonary Resuscitation
CQ10: Coenzyme Q10
CRT: Cardiac Resynchronization Therapy
CRT-D: Cardiac Resynchronization Therapy Device
    (pacemaker)
CT: Computed Tomography
CTA: Computed Tomography Angiogram
CV: Coronary Vein
CVA: Cerebrovascular Accident
CVC: Central Venous Catheter
CVI: Cerebrovascular Incident
CVD: Cardiovascular Disease
CVP: Central Venous Pressure
DBP: Diastolic Blood Pressure
DCM: Dilated Cardiomyopathy
DIL: Diltiazem
DVT: Deep Vein Thrombosis
EAT: Ectopic Atrial Tachycardia
EBCT: Electron Beam Computed Tomography
ECD: Endocardial Cushion Defect
ECG: Electrocardiogram
    (also the original Greek EKG, electrokardiogram)
EF: Ejection Fraction
EFA: Essential Fatty Acid
EGD: Esophagogastroduodenoscopy
EKG: Electrokardiogram
    (often anglicized to ECG, electrocardiogram)
EMC: Encephalomyocarditis
EMF: Endomyocardial Fibrosis
EP: Electrophysiologist
    (or Electrophysiology, as in "EP study")
EPS: Electrophysiology Study
EVH: Endoscopic Vessel Harvesting

FFP: Fresh Frozen Plasma
FFR: Fractional Flow Reservoir
FIRM: Focal Impulse and Rotor Modulation
GERD: Gastro-esophageal Reflux Disease
HBP: High Blood Pressure (hypertension)
HC: High Cholesterol
HCM: Hypertrophic Cardiomyopathy
HCTZ: Hydrochlorothiazide
HDL: High Density Lipoprotein
HOCM: Hypertrophic Obstructive Cardiomyopathy
HTN: Hypertension (high blood pressure)
IABP: Intra-Aortic Balloon Pump
IAD: Implantable Atrial Defibrillator
IAS: Interatrial Seprtum
IC: Intracardiac
ICD: Implantable Cardioverter-Defibrillator
ICG: Impedance Cardiography
ICM: Implantable Cardiac Monitor
IDC: Idiopathic Dilated Cardiomyopathy
IE: Infective Endocarditis
IHD: Ischemic Heart Disease
IHSS: Idiopathic Hypertrophic Subaortic Stenosis
ILM: Implantable Loop Monitor
ILR: Implantable Loop Recorder
INR: International Normalized Ratio
IST: Inappropriate Sinus Tachycardia
IVS: Interventricular Septum
JET: Junctional Ectopic Tachycardia
JRT: Junctional Reciprocating Tachycardia
LA: Left Atrium
LAA: Left Atrial Appendage
LAD: Left Anterior Descending (coronary artery) or
        Left Axis Deviation
LAF: Lone Atrial Fibrillation
LAFB: Left Anterior Fascicular Block
LAHB: Left Anterior Hemiblock
LAP: Left Arterial Pressure
LBBB: Left Branch Bundle Block
LC: Left Circumflex (artery)

Appendix

LCA: Left Coronary Artery
LDH: Lactic Dehydrogenase
LDL: Low Density Lipoprotein
LFHB: Left Fascicular Hemiblock
LHC: Left Heart Catheterization
LIMA: Left Internal Mammary Artery
LM: Left Main (artery)
LPFB: Left Posterior Fascicular Block
LQT: Long QT
LQTS: Long QT Syndrome
LV: Left Ventricle
LVAD: Left Ventricular Assist Device
LVEDP: Left Ventricular End-Diastolic Pressure
LVEDR: Left Ventricular End-Diastolic Radius
LVEF: Left Ventricular Ejection Fraction
LVH: Left Ventricular Hypertrophy
LVNC: Left Ventricular Noncompaction Cardiomyopathy
LVOT: Left Ventricular Outflow Tract
LVOTO: Left Ventricular Outflow Tract Obstruction
LVOTT: Left Ventricular Outflow Tract Tachycardia
M: heart murmur
MAP: Mean Arterial Pressure
MAT: Multifocal Atrial Tachycardia (same as WAP)
MCL: Midclavicular Line
MI: Myocardial Infarction or
      Myocardial Insufficiency
MIDCAB: Minimally Invasive Coronary Artery Bypass Graft
MRA: Magnetic Resonance Angiogram
MRI: Magnetic Resonance Imaging
MS: Mitral Stenosis
MUGA: Multiple Gated Acquisition scanning
MV: Mitral Valve
MVD: Coronary Microvascular Disease
MVP: Mitral Valve Prolapse
MVPS: Mitral Valve Prolapse Syndrome
NBTE: Nonbacterial Thrombotic Endocarditis
NCC: Noncompaction Cardiomyopathy
NCS: Neurocardiogenic Syndrome
NOA: Novel Oral Anticoagulant

Appendix

NSAID: Non-Steroidal Anti-Inflammatory Drug
NSR: Normal Sinus Rhythm
NST: Nonsinus Tachycardia
NSTEMI: Non-ST-Elevation Myocardial Infarction
NSVT: Nonsustained Ventricular Tachycardia
NTG: Nitroglycerin
O2: oxygen
PA: Pulmonary Arterial (line) or
        Pulmonary Artery (pressure)
PAC: Premature Atrial Contraction
PACAB: Port-Access Coronary Artery Bypass
PAD: Peripheral Artery Disease
PAF: Paroxysmal Atrial Fibrillation
PAP: Pulmonary Arterial Pressure
PAT: Paroxysmal Atrial Tachycardia
PCC: Prothrombin Complex Concentrate
PCI: Percutaneous Coronary Intervention
PCO2: partial pressure of carbon dioxide
PDA: Patent Ductus Arteriosis
PE: Pulmonary Embolism
PET: Positron Emission Tomography
PFO: Patent Forman Ovale (a hole in the intra-atrial septum)
PH: Pulmonary Hypertension
PJRT: Permanent Junctional Reciprocating Tachycardia
PMI: Point of Maximum Impulse
PMR: Percutaneous Myocardial Revascularization
PO2: partial pressure of oxygen
PortCAB: Port-Access Coronary Artery Bypass
POTS: Postural Orthostatic Tachycardia Syndrome
PPI: Proton Pump Inhibitor
PPCM: Peripartum Cardiomyopathy
PRN: Pro Re Nata (or "as needed")
PST: Paroxysmal Sinus Tachycardia
PSVT: Paroxysmal Supraventricular Tachyacardia
PT: Prothrombin Time
PTCA: Percutaneous Transluminal Coronary Angioplasty
PTT: Partial Thromboplastin Time
PV: Pulmonary Vein
PVC: Premature Ventricular Contraction

Appendix

PVI: Pulmonary Vein Isolation
PWP: Pulmonary Wedge Pressure
QD: per day
QID: four times a day
QRS: ventricular depolarization time
QRST or QT: duration of ventricular electrical activity
RA: Right Atrium
RAA: Right Atrial Appendage
RAFB: Right Anterior Fascicular Block
RAHB: Right Anterior Hemiblock
RBBB: Right Branch Bundle Block
RCA: Right Coronary Artery
RCM: Restrictive Cardiomyopathy
RFA: Radiofrequency Ablation
RFHB: Right Fascicular Hemiblock
RHC: Right Heart Catheterization
RHD: Rheumatic Heart Disease
RIMA: Right Internal Mammary Artery
RNVG: Radionuclide Ventrialography
RPFB: Right Posterior Fascicular Block
RSA: Respiratory Sinus Arrhythmia
RV: Right Ventricle
RVAD: Right Ventricular Assist Device
RVEDP: Right Ventricular End-Diastolic Pressure
RVEDR: Right Ventricular End-Diastolic Radius
RVOT: Right Ventricular Outflow Tract
RVOTO: Right Ventricular Outflow Tract Obstruction
RVOTT: Right Ventricular Outflow Tract Tachycardia
RVR: Rapid Ventricular Response (or Rate)
SA: Sinoatrial (as in "SA node")
SB: Sinus Bradycardia
SBE: Subacute Bacterial Endocarditis
SBP: Systolic Blood Pressure
SCB: Sodium Channel Blocker
SCD: Sudden Cardiac Death
SNRT: Sinoatrial Node Reentrant Tachycardia
SOB: Shortness of Breath
SPECT: Single-Photon Emission Computed Tomography
ST: Sinus Tachycardia

STEMI: ST-Elevation Myocardial Infarction
SVT: Supraventricular Tachycardia or
        Sustained Ventricular Tachycardia
TAH: Total Artificial Heart
TEE: Transesophageal Echocardiogram
Tg: Triglycerides
TIA: Transient Ischemic Attack
TID: three times a day
TMR: Transmyocardial Revascularization
TOE: Transesophageal Echocardiogram
TTE: Transthoracic Echocardiogram
TTR: Time in Therapeutic Range
TTE: Transthoracic Echocardiogram
tPA: Tissue Plasminogen Activator
TV: Tricuspid Valve
UA: Unstable Angina
UPPP: Uvulopaletopharyngoplasty
USA: Unstable Angina
VAD: Ventricular Assist Device
VB: Ventricular Bigeminy
VE: Ventricular Ectopy
VEB: Ventricular Ectopic Beats
VF: Ventricular Fibrillation
Vfib, V-fib: Ventricular Fibrillation
VLDL: Very Low Density Lipoprotein
VPB: Ventricular Premature Beat
VPC: Ventricular Premature Complexes
VS: Ventricular Salvo
VSA: Ventricular Septal Aneurysm
VSD: Ventricular Septal Defect
VSR: Ventricular Septal Rupture
VT: Ventricular Tachycardia
VTn: Nonsustained Ventricular Tachycardia
VTs: Sustained Ventricular Tachycardia
Vtach, V-tach: Ventricular Tachycardia
WAP: Wandering Atrial Pacemaker (same as MAT)
WPW: Wolff-Parkinson-White Syndrome

Appendix

Antiarrhythmic Agents

Class I – Sodium Channel Blockers
Reduce the sensitivity of the individual heart muscle fibers to rapid electrical impulses.

Examples include:
Ia) *Disopyramide, Procainamide, Quinidine*
Ib) *Lidocaine, Mexiletine, Phenytoin, Tocainide*
Ic) *Encainide, Flecainide, Moricizine, Propafenone*

Class II – Beta Blockers
Reduce the entire heart's response to epinephrine (adrenaline) and other stress-related hormones.

Examples include:
Acebutolol, Atenolol, Betaxolol, Bisoprolol, Carteolol, Carvedilol, Esmolol, Labetalol, Metoprolol, Nadolol, Penbutolol, Propranolol, Timolol

Class III – Potassium Channel Blockers
Prolong the heart muscle's refractory period (the period during which it does not respond to electrical impulses).

Examples include:
Amiodarone, Dofetilide, Dronedarone, Ibutilide, Sotalol

Class IV – Calcium Channel Blockers
Slow the conduction of electrical impulses throughout the heart muscle.

Examples include:
Diltiazem, Verapamil, all drugs ending in "-dipine"

Class V – Other
Act by some other means (possibly unknown).

Examples include:
Adenosine, Digitoxin/Digoxin, Magnesium Sulfate

Made in the USA
San Bernardino, CA
15 June 2015